The Lonely American

The Lonely American

Drifting Apart
in the
Twenty-first
Century

Jacqueline Olds, M.D., and Richard S. Schwartz, M.D.

Beacon Press
Boston

Beacon Press
25 Beacon Street
Boston, Massachusetts 02108-2892
www.beacon.org

Beacon Press books
are published under the auspices of
the Unitarian Universalist Association of Congregations.

12 11 10 09 8 7 6 5 4 3 2 1

This book is printed on acid-free paper that meets the uncoated paper
ANSI/NISO specifications for permanence as revised in 1992.

Text design by Yvonne Tsang at Wilsted and Taylor Publishing Services

Library of Congress Cataloging-in-Publication Data

Olds, Jacqueline.
  The lonely American : drifting apart in the twenty-first century /
Jacqueline Olds and Richard S. Schwartz.
      p. cm.
  Includes bibliographical references and index.
  ISBN-13: 978-0-8070-0034-2 (hardcover : alk. paper)
    1. Social isolation—United States. 2. Loneliness—United States.
I. Schwartz, Richard (Richard S.) II. Title.

HM1131.O43 2008
302.5'45097309051—dc22   2008019339

To our parents,
our children,
and our friends,
who have kept us
from being lonely

Contents

CHAPTER 1

The Elephant in the Room

Americans in the twenty-first century devote more technology to staying connected than any society in history, yet somehow the devices fail us: studies show that we feel increasingly alone. Our lives are spent in a tug-of-war between conflicting desires— we want to stay connected, and we want to be free. We lurch back and forth, reaching for both, and are surprised by our sadness when one side actually wins. How much of one should we give up in order to have more of the other? How do we know when we've got it right?

This argument probably began as soon as language made it possible for groups to argue, but it is also a particularly American controversy. Over the last decade, the debate about freedom and connection in the United States has leaped from rarely read doctoral dissertations to front-page national news. What caught people's attention was a series of alarms, given in the form of data-driven studies, suggesting that our society is in the midst of a dramatic and progressive slide toward disconnection. Robert Putnam's *Bowling Alone* was the loudest alarm, combining extensive data on the fraying of social connections with a powerful thesis demonstrating the importance of social networks to a healthy democracy. The book struck a chord and seemingly endless public debate about whether or not Putnam was ignoring new forms of connection that were every bit as effective as the waning old forms. Questions ranged from the trivial (don't burgeoning youth-soccer leagues matter as much as disappearing bowling leagues?) to the technological (what about the Internet and cell phones?).

These issues were brought into sharp focus recently by two major studies. In the first, using data from the General Social Survey (GSS), a group headed by Duke University researcher Miller McPherson found that between 1985 and 2004, the number of people with whom the average American discussed "important matters" dropped from three to two. Even more stunning, the number of people who said there was *no one* with whom they discussed important matters tripled: in 2004, individuals without a single confidant now made up nearly a quarter of those surveyed.[1] Our country is now filled with them. For readers who remain skeptical, it is worth noting that the authors of the study themselves were skeptics. They were surprised by their own results; they had expected to prove Putnam wrong.

The second study was the 2000 U.S. census. One of the most remarkable facts to emerge from this census is that one out of every four households consists of one person only. The number of one-person households has been increasing steadily since 1940, when they accounted for roughly 7 percent of households; today, there are more people living alone than at any point in U.S. history.[2] Placing the census data and the General Social Survey side by side, the evidence that this country is in the midst of a major social change is overwhelming.

The significance of this increased aloneness is amplified by a very different body of research. There is now a clear consensus among medical researchers that social connection has powerful effects on health. Socially connected people live longer, respond better to stress, have more robust immune systems, and do better at fighting a variety of specific illnesses. These medical benefits derive directly from the social connection itself, not just from lifestyle improvements, such as better diet, more exercise, and better medical care, that might go along with it. Putnam argues that social connection is good for the country. Medical research has clearly demonstrated that social connection is good for individual health. Yet people in this country continue to drift apart. We want to understand why.

In 1970, the sociologist Philip Slater published a powerful book called *The Pursuit of Loneliness*. Slater wrote:

> We seek a private house, a private means of transportation, a private garden, a private laundry, self-service stores, and do-it-yourself skills of every kind. An enormous technology seems to have set itself the task of making it unnecessary for one human being ever to ask anything of another in the course of going about his daily business. Even within the family Americans are unique in their feeling that each member should have a separate room, and even a separate telephone, television, and car when economically possible. We seek more and more privacy, and feel more and more alienated and lonely when we get it.[3]

When Slater looked at the America of his day, he saw people who actively sought the very things that made them unhappy and bitter. He also asked why, but his answer got stuck in its particular historical moment. He wrote at the height of the Vietnam War, a time of increasingly intense confrontation between a mix of countercultural student radicals and hippies and what Slater labeled the "old culture." Much of the book is a brilliant rant against the dominant culture by a writer who believed that society was poised on the brink of cataclysmic transformation. His subtitle was *American Culture at the Breaking Point*, but after more than four decades, nothing has broken. What we have instead is more of the same—

more isolation (and more objective data on that isolation), more longing for connection, and more technology that promises better connections but never quite delivers. It is time to revisit Slater's questions and seek answers for our own time.

We came, and still come, to these questions as psychiatrists. Our first concern was the welfare of our patients: we began to notice how much of their suffering was bound up in isolation and loneliness, whatever other diagnostic labels might be applied to them. We began to notice how hard it was for our patients to talk about their isolation, which seemed to fill them with deep shame. We began to notice that most of our patients were more comfortable saying they were *depressed* than saying they were *lonely*. Somehow, while our culture has successfully destigmatized mental illness (at least a little), it has restigmatized an ordinary human emotion. Finally, we began to notice versions of the same suffering around us in friends, family, and acquaintances, and, again, what puzzled us more than the disconnection itself was an almost reflexive denial that it mattered. Someone would talk at length and with great sadness about losing contact with formerly close family members and friends, and then the whole subject would be shrugged off as if it were just a minor inconvenience in a typically busy life. The word *lonely* was determinedly avoided, yet the denial of loneliness is horribly self-defeating. Health and happiness, the two things we all say matter most, are certifiably linked to social connectedness.

We first wrote about these issues more than a decade ago in a book called *Overcoming Loneliness in Everyday Life*. Since our goal then was to offer practical help, we spoke only briefly about the cultural roots of the problem. That is the question we tackle now, as Philip Slater did forty years ago. The leading emotion in Slater's writing was clearly anger. Ours is probably sadness, since we come to the question steeped in the unhappiness of individuals. But, like Slater, we are hopeful about the possibility of change, and, like

Slater, we will focus on the dynamic interaction between social forces and individual psychology. We will bring together sociologists' studies of social networks and connection with a very different kind of data that our patients share with us. Many of the stories we hear open a window into the hidden motives and quiet decisions that lead people (often inadvertently) toward greater social disconnection. Many of the stories are about feeling left out, an experience that seems easy to dismiss as trivial or even childish. We will add to the mix an emerging understanding of the evolutionary significance and neurobiology of feeling left out, an understanding that helps to make sense of its central role as an engine of human emotion and behavior.

The elephant in the room is loneliness, even if the room is a psychiatrist's office. As psychiatrists, we deal with depression every day; it is the bread and butter of our professional lives. But depression has become a catchall complaint for everyone from the stay-at-home mother who talks only to toddlers all day to the angry unemployed man who feels the world has handed him a raw deal; the diagnosis may be accurate, but the stories people tell to explain how they arrived at their unhappy conditions are often wrong. At this moment in history, it is fashionable to talk about a "chemical imbalance," but that label is not as illuminating as many people assume. Every thought and every emotion involves changes in electrochemical signals in the brain; therefore, all states of feeling can be regarded as chemical imbalances. What gets lost in this perspective is the complicated relationship between depression and social isolation. What gets lost is the story of a mother who grows depressed simply because she has no adults to talk to, and the story of an unemployed man who feels completely left out because his entire social world had consisted of daily contact with his coworkers.

We argue that a great many people who think of themselves as depressed have in fact a sense of isolation at the core of their feelings. Unfortunately, talking about loneliness in America is deeply stigmatized; we see ourselves as a self-reliant people who do not whine about neediness. If a person is going to complain, far better to complain about what someone has done to him (abuse, coercion, rejection) or what diagnoses and addictions he was saddled with; to wistfully describe how lonely he feels is simply not socially acceptable. Because of this persistent stigma, we as psychiatrists often learn about our patients' isolation almost by accident, long after they've received the diagnoses they wanted, such as depression, anxiety, and posttraumatic stress disorder. Their stories can help us understand the stark facts of sociologists' surveys and bridge the gap between individual choice and nationwide change. The embarrassment that our patients feel about their loneliness, an embarrassment that leads them to hide their loneliness until we ask the right questions (and ask them tactfully), also helps us make sense of seemingly contradictory sociological data.

We sometimes wonder if the GSS stumbled across the evidence of increasing social isolation almost by accident, as we did —in other words, by asking the right questions in a safe setting. At about the same time that Miller McPherson and his colleagues were using data from the GSS to show that aloneness was increasing in America, the Pew Internet and American Life Project, asking different questions, came to the opposite conclusion.[4] The Pew researchers (Jeffrey Boase and others from the University of Toronto) argued that social networks are flourishing in America. In *their* survey, the average American reported fifteen very close core ties and sixteen somewhat close ties. The Pew Project contacted people by telephone and asked, "How many people are you very close to?" and "How many people are you somewhat close to?" Given the heroic efforts by so many of our patients to camouflage their loneliness, we are not surprised that the standard response to a telephone interview was the equivalent of "Oh, I have lots of friends." By contrast, GSS used face-to-face interviews and asked, "From time to time, most people discuss important matters with other people. Looking back over the last six months, who are the people with whom you discussed matters important to you? Just tell me their first names or initials."[5] The question neatly sidesteps the issue of whether you have friends and whether anyone likes you. It also makes it harder to come up with a comfortingly high number on the spot.[6]

Whatever the precise numbers, the GSS data makes clear that something important is changing in Americans' relationships with one another, and that change is leaving a very large number of people very much alone. We see some of them as patients, and we see many more around us. We want to understand how an isolation that almost no one really wants ends up engulfing so many people, and how it affects them as individuals and all of us as a country. As practicing psychiatrists, we realize that this inquiry is not in line with our business interests. Most patients want medical diagnoses and pills or psychotherapy, and the job of paid confidant to lonely people is a reliable source of income for most psychotherapists. These treatments often do help bring people back into the world of connections with others. But the buy-your-way-out-of-it approach that is so much a part of modern American life is not a very efficient way of dealing with a national trend. We would rather address the trend itself, which seems to be creating a lemming-like walk into loneliness.

We, the authors, should identify ourselves further. We are married to each other and have been for almost thirty years; writing about loneliness and connection without mentioning that fact seems absurd. If it is hard to tease out two separate voices in these chapters, it is probably because we have shared so much more than the writing process over the last quarter of a century. (We also wrote *Marriage in Motion*, a book about lasting marriages, together—a high-risk move. Since our marriage survived that project, we are optimistic about this one.) However, in our early years,

each of us had a very different personal experience with what we
believe is a universal dilemma—the tension between freedom and
connection. Jacqueline grew up in an academic family that moved
from university to university, and she was repeatedly stripped of
friends and placed in the role of the new kid in class. Richard grew
up as an only child in a three-generation household, and he was so
constantly surrounded by family that outside connections sometimes seemed superfluous. We arrive at our critique fully embedded in the confusions of the culture that we criticize.

The starting point for almost every contemporary examina-
tion of disconnection in America is Alexis de Tocqueville's 1835
observation that the United States had struck a dynamic balance
between individualism and community. The country was thriving,
but Tocqueville feared for its future. Here are some of his most famous words (which we quote a bit nervously; a reviewer in the *New
York Times* recently warned readers away from any book that starts
with Tocqueville):

> Individualism is a calm considered feeling which disposes
> each citizen to isolate himself from the mass of his fel-
> lows and withdraw into the circle of family and friends;
> with this little society formed to his taste, he gladly leaves
> the greater society to look after itself...They form the
> habit of thinking of themselves in isolation and imagine
> that their whole destiny is in their hands...[Finally] each
> man is forever thrown back on himself and there is the dan-
> ger that he may be shut up in the solitude of his own heart.[7]

Upon those words, a series of critiques of overexuberant individualism have been built. Slater's is one of them. A decade ago, our
own attempt to examine the roots of isolation in America also focused on the tilt toward excessive individualism; the country was,
after all, settled by tie breakers, individuals who were willing to

sever ties with surrounding communities and even families to cross the ocean or press westward. Initially, the sheer hardship of building a life in a new land enforced a balance between individualism and interdependence, but as life got easier, the balance did not hold.

We still believe that premise, but in the intervening years, we have begun to examine another powerful shaping force that stands at or near the center of our culture's aspirations and fears: the myth of the outsider. More accurately, this is a cluster of tightly knit and contradictory myths about standing apart. They range from the loner who masters things on his own terms without help from family or social connections to the left-out misfit who never gets picked for the team. The positive pole of these ideas is an updated version of Emerson's self-reliant American, a cherished part of our national identity. The negative pole is the loser who desperately wants to fit in but can't. When you stand at the positive pole, you stand alone. When you stand at the negative pole, you feel lonely and left out.

This book is our attempt to tease out the consequences of these myths in twenty-first-century American life. Like all powerful myths, they operate at the boundary between society's cherished values and an individual's concrete choices. Like all powerful myths, they shape one's conscious and unconscious choices. And, like the most interesting myths, they hold together conflicting wishes. For we, both as a society and as individuals, are deeply ambivalent about the outsider. It is precisely this ambivalence about standing apart, the confused and unacknowledged feelings about it, that leads people to actively seek the very things that leave them unhappy, bitter, and increasingly alone.

An easy place to begin exploring these strong but confused feelings about standing apart is the U.S. presidential campaign. Each candidate competes for the most prized starting position: the political outsider. The label most likely to sink a candidate like a stone is "Washington insider." It is a curious spectacle, the most powerfully connected men and women in the country repeatedly presenting themselves to the public as disconnected mavericks. The artist as romanticized outsider is also a reliable promotional tool in music, literature, and the visual arts. And of course, there is the lonesome-cowboy hero of so many cherished Westerns. The entrepreneur as contemporary business hero is heir to the same tradition, an outsider by choice who beats the insiders at their own game.

The flip side to the story is that everyone hates to feel left out. Look at young children playing together: the most likely moment for an explosion of tears or rage is when a child feels left out. Look at the long history of using exile as one of the worst punishments that can be imposed on an individual. Look at the somewhat more recent history of using the powerful technique of shunning as a method of punishment and social control. We can even revisit the famous Oedipal crisis of early childhood—the moment when a child becomes aware that his parents have a connection with each other from which he is excluded. Freud described the crisis in sexual terms, but more broadly and probably more powerfully, this is the moment of a child's first, traumatic awareness of being left out in a way that really matters.

Our culture currently views isolating behaviors as marks of high status. Slater described some of them forty years ago, but today we have even more. There are so many more possessions and technologies that each individual must have for himself rather than share with others. There is the rising status of being too busy to chat or even to answer the telephone; it is so much more efficient to have a machine take a message and then respond in one's own good time, or resort to the silence of e-mail. Somewhat ironically, but in a similar vein, people sometimes answer their cell phones no matter what else they might be doing, sacrificing the connections of the moment to prove that they have even more im-

portant connections in their lives. There is the privilege of working from home when possible (or, even better, from the peaceful
solitude of a vacation home), connected by e-mail but deprived of
the casual conversations and shared moments that most people
like best about the workplace. People feel they are so much more
likely to be productive and creative this way. Virginia Woolf eloquently proclaimed the importance of "a room of one's own." She
also walked into a river with stones in her pockets.

It is curious that people put so much energy into isolating
themselves and are then completely unprepared for how it makes
them feel. And in those moments of feeling down, the cultural
stigma of loneliness comes into play. The heroic outsider thrives
in states of aloneness; only losers feel lonely. Only losers don't get
picked for the teams, don't have dates when they want them, don't
have people with whom they can discuss important matters—so
we each keep our loneliness to ourselves, not even wanting to tell
therapists about it, and become even more alone in our shame.

Here is the crux of our argument: people in our society drift
away from social connections because of both a push and a pull.
The push is the frenetic, overscheduled, hypernetworked intensity of modern life. The pull is the American pantheon of self-
reliant heroes who stand apart from the crowd. As a culture, we all
romanticize standing apart and long to have destiny in our own
hands. But as individuals, each of us hates feeling left out. In the
interplay between these conflicting goals, our society has fallen
into a trap, one that has been made even more inescapable by an
abundance of technologies that ostensibly provide better tools for
connection. In examining this duality, we will review the stubborn
stigma attached to ordinary loneliness. We will discuss what Barbara Ehrenreich called the "cult of busyness," with its vicious
cycle of staying busy to avoid seeming lonely and feeling lonely
because there seems to be no time to cultivate relationships. We
will look at the ripple effects of social isolation on areas as var-

ied as physical health, children's emotional problems, substance abuse, and even global warming. We will look at the impact of progressive social disconnection on the institution of marriage. Throughout the book, we will draw on the myth of standing apart, in all its rich contradictions, as we search for a new way of handling the perpetual tension between freedom and connection, a way that we hope speaks directly to our place and our time.

CHAPTER 2

Frantic without a Peep

Busyness as a Virtue and a Curse

The social lives of Americans are changing. Ordinary wishes are reshaping ordinary lives in remarkable ways. Perfectly reasonable people with no particular emotional problems are retreating from the tumult of social contact that, until recently, formed the fabric of almost everyone's daily life. The retreat is a quiet one, a set of small steps back rather than a dramatic dropping-out. The wishes behind those steps seem simple and understandable—a little more peace and quiet, a little more privacy in a hectic and intrusive world, a little less stress. Many of the changes signal high social status, because the opportunity to make them goes along with prosperity, job seniority, and access to the latest technology. Living in an affluent neighborhood where you never see your neighbors is a simple example, but there are many smaller steps, like working from home rather than spending the day surrounded by coworkers in an office or a factory, or shopping at home rather than rubbing elbows with other customers and live salespeople at a market. But along with giving a respite from a frantic world, these small steps are turning into an overall drift toward self-inflicted loneliness. Stepping back from the fray leads to a surprising result—the experience of being left out. The effect of that experience on individual lives and on American society as a whole is surprisingly far-reaching.

Talk to Americans about their lives and one thing you will hear over and over again is how busy most people feel. People complain about being too busy, but if you listen closely, you will hear that people are proud of their busyness. It serves as a badge of toughness, success, and importance. When most people talk about how busy they are, it is simultaneously a complaint and a boast.

We Americans are rightly proud of our tendency to use our time productively. We have happily described ourselves as an industrious nation, a nation of doers—energetic, ambitious, competitive. In the Middle Ages, there was an important theological debate about the relative merits of the active life and the contemplative life. Arguments in favor of the contemplative life never really took hold in the New World. An American life is an active life. All that activity has accumulated over the years to make this the most prosperous country in the world.

Americans are not resting on their laurels either. On both macro and micro levels, companies and individuals constantly try to find ways to use time more productively. These efforts are not always the result of free choice. Once this continuous striving was driven by the demands of wresting a home from the wilderness. Now it's driven by the threats of international competition and, on an individual level, by just trying to keep up. As various authors have pointed out, a middle-class family could live comfortably on a single salary in the 1970s, whereas it now takes two working parents to sustain that same standard of living.[1] But this country's citizens have literally made a virtue out of necessity. Productivity is a virtue in America. Busyness itself is a virtue in America. And because busyness is virtuous, it has "legs." When necessity recedes, the busyness does not stop. It continues not only because it is a habit but because it is a "good" habit. And since busyness is a public virtue, a boast as well as a complaint, since people want to be

seen as virtuous even in those moments when their virtues are flag-
ging, they sometimes present a façade of busyness to the world
whether they are being productive or not. Barbara Ehrenreich
captured something essential about our culture with her phrase *the
cult of busyness*.[2] The elevation of busyness itself to a virtue has had
profound social consequences. It affects the social fabric of the
country and the daily choices of individuals whether or not this really is an unusually busy age. But before we examine those effects,
we must ask, How busy are we?

The Overworked American?

In 1992, the economist Juliet Schor published a book that sparked
a vigorous and ongoing debate. In *The Overworked American*,
Schor used government statistics as evidence that Americans were
spending more time at paid work in the late 1980s than they did
in the late 1960s—on average, an additional 163 hours per year.[3]
Both women and men were working longer hours, but the increase
for women was much larger. There is a continuing controversy
about how to interpret complex data—how reliable workers' reports of their hours are, how variable their workweeks are, and
how to make sense of data that mixes workers in different family circumstances and at different points in their lives. Some economists claim that work hours are actually decreasing. In the midst
of this confusion, an important perspective is offered by two
Berkeley sociologists, Michael Hout and Caroline Hanley. With
the dramatic increase in married women's participation in the
workforce, the *combined* work hours of husbands and wives grew
by twelve or thirteen hours per week between 1968 and 2001.[4]
Perhaps a better name for this phenomenon is, as these sociologists call it, the overworked *family*.[5]

When we shift our attention from paid work to just work, plain
and simple, the sense of exhaustion increases. On average, each
parent in dual-earner families works about fifteen hours a day

on the combination of paid work and family chores, leading to seventy-five hours of work per week.[6] This rising burden explains how Americans can have more leisure time (meaning "time away from paid work") than they did a generation ago and yet still feel more frantic than ever.

Another important window on attitudes toward work as well as hours spent working is offered by data on vacations. American workers gave back, or didn't take advantage of, 574 million vacation days in 2005, the equivalent of more than twenty thousand lifetimes. Surveys done by Gallup and the Conference Board indicate that Americans, who already take fewer vacation days than workers in any other industrial nation in the world, are cutting back even further. About 25 percent of Americans get no paid vacation time, and another 33 percent will take only a seven-day vacation.[7] The average American may or may not be busier than ever before but is certainly not a slacker. Americans still find virtue in work, productivity, and simply being busy.

A Very Busy Couple

Alan and Ginny have been friends of ours for many years. Their career paths (they are both lawyers) have not always been smooth. They have each faced some surprising twists and turns and a few discouraging dead ends, but, as they approach their sixties, they are clearly successful, with clients lined up far into the future waiting for their expert advice and guidance. They are also very busy. They work long hours and bring work home and still feel perpetually guilty about all the work that remains undone. They want to continue working. They probably *have* to continue working. But they also wanted some relief.

Their answer was to find a refuge, a farmhouse in northern New Hampshire that was far away from all the reminders of work and that had a rhythm of life all its own. For the first time in their lives, they bought a second home and threw themselves into it.

They began spending almost every weekend there, leaving early on Fridays (which of course required them to work even longer hours Monday through Thursday). Alan learned to mow their meadow with an old-fashioned scythe, backbreaking work but blissfully different from lawyering. Their beautiful second home —one of the great emblems of success in American life—was a haven for them, and they were happy.

Several years later, Alan and Ginny began to talk to us about what they had noticed slipping away from them. They no longer felt as connected to friends and neighbors. Splitting their lives between two communities, they felt not quite part of either one. Weekends in New Hampshire provided a much more relaxing alternative to all the social obligations they faced when they spent their weekends in Boston, but it turned out that all those social obligations, which had seemed like unwelcome additions to the busyness of their lives, also kept them connected to people they cared about. They still loved their farmhouse. They would still have made the same choice again. There was just a new wistfulness as they talked about their lives.

Talking longer, deep into the night, all four of us doing our best to reconnect, a certain darkness of thought emerged along with the wistfulness. There were feelings of being left out, turned away, and discarded by friends who no longer bothered to call, friends who, they'd heard, had moved on to new friends. Alan and Ginny, though they had chosen to leave, were just a little angry that they were being left out. When we de-stress by stepping away from the constant press of demands, all of us can find ourselves a little wistful and a little angry about being left out. Friends, relatives, and neighbors continue with their lives, looking happily connected to one another. Anger, envy, resentment can enter into the picture—even though the disengagement was an active choice. Alan and Ginny are thoughtful about their lives. They understood their own role in creating their predicament. Most people have no sense at all that they've been sending out signals that they want privacy and solitude. Instead of talking this out with friends, most people just take another step back, usually accompanied by some version of the thought *Well, at least if I'm alone, I can have things my own way.* Soon they are set in their ways—or to put it a little less charitably, they develop the habit of not compromising on their particular desires. Sharing and compromise go out the window. They sing some modern version of the old Billie Holiday song "God Bless the Child (That's Got His Own)."

You Can Do Anything You Want

Alan and Ginny had set about trying to solve the problem of busyness by adding something new to their lives. They added a place of refuge, but what came along with it was a set of new responsibilities and activities to shoehorn into their already too-busy weeks. Something had to give, and what slipped away was a piece of the social fabric of their lives. We can argue about whether the trade-off was worth it. Perhaps it was. But we need to pay attention to the trade-off. One of the great American myths is that people can engineer lives without trade-offs, that they can have it all. Americans may be the only people in the world who believe that each individual has the right and the capacity to fit whatever he or she wants into one small life. Examples abound. Women (like one of the authors of this book) feel that there is no conflict in trying to be a physician, a spouse, a mother, and a writer. Actors retire and become civics teachers in middle age. On a recent radio show, the author of a book on aging baby boomers chided a caller, a retired man who'd wondered whether it was too late to start a Ph.D. program since he'd be too old to get a university teaching job when he finished. The author's response was essentially "We are never too old." America is the original "You can be anything you want if you really try, and it's never too late to start trying!" country.

People's unwillingness to say no to themselves fuels their frenetic busyness. They don't know their limits. In fact, Americans are not supposed to have limits; limits are for the faint of heart. That is what our children are supposed to be taught, setting them up for frantic lives of their own. There doesn't seem to be an icon of good parenting who says, "Well, you can't do everything, dear. It's one or the other." Nowadays, a parent who says something like that to children would be seen as raining on their parade, suppressing their nascent creativity and drive. Jacqueline was once asked to give a talk on child development to a group of Sunday-school teachers. Soon the discussion turned to the teachers' main complaint: the parents of their pupils did not seem to know how to teach priorities to their children. The religious teachers felt they had to compete with athletics, academic tutoring, dance lessons, music lessons, and all the other random skill lessons that took place on Sunday mornings. Now, some might argue that religion should be on a par with all these competing concerns, but these Sunday-school teachers certainly did not see it that way. They felt that parents, even those parents who sent their children to Sunday school, had stopped trying to teach their children that some kinds of learning were more important than others. The school was filled with children whose parents were teaching them to fill their lives with activities but not that some kinds of busyness mattered more than others.

Some of the determination to add even more busyness to already busy lives comes because most mothers have jobs and because many fathers want to be more involved with their children than their own fathers were with them. In the novel *I Don't Know How She Does It*, Allison Pearson created a hilarious send-up of women who wish not just to do it all but to do it all *best*. The book is set in England, but Pearson decided to write it after reading a stress survey of American women in *Good Housekeeping*. She summarized the survey like this: "It said that all that most working women wanted for Mother's Day was a bit of time to themselves. It also said they were too tired to have sex with their husbands and felt they were failing both at work and as a parent."[8] Pearson starts her novel with a scene in which a mother is trying to "distress" a store-bought pie that she's taking to the school social night so the other mothers will think the pie is homemade. Most mothers we know laugh out loud while reading it. The competitive tension among parents about whose children are doing the best is another major stress on both parents and children that Pearson portrays well. A woman who is too busy already with both a career and a family will find that there are always people doing a better job than her at one or the other, if only because they are not trying to do both. It is a simple point but offers little consolation.

Men feel that if they want to make contributions at home (or if their wives expect them to make contributions at home), they'll have little time for seeing same-sex friends, except perhaps on the sidelines of children's sports events. In a study we did some years ago, the main spontaneous regret we heard from working fathers with young children was that they had lost contact with their male friends.[9] As one man in our practice put it, "My wife and I are in survival mode all week, and then in the evenings and weekends, we just want to flop." Flopping usually means watching TV or a DVD. In other words, flopping takes you just as far away from friends, relatives, and neighbors as a regular weekend trip to New Hampshire.

The irony is that even when people are flopping alone because they feel too busy the rest of the time, they stay rather busy while they flop. With the wonders of new technology, even flopping offers the opportunity for multitasking. What with checking e-mail, instant messaging, ordering takeout, shopping online, and watching taped or Tivoed shows, there is quite a lot to be done. We Americans escape from busyness into more busyness. It is our pride as well as our curse.

Busyness as a Virtue

A good friend described the impact of busyness on our neighborhoods brilliantly. "Being neighborly used to mean visiting people. Now being nice to your neighbors means not bothering them." People's lives are shaped by how busy they are. Lives are also shaped by the respect and deference that is given to busyness—especially when it is valued above the potentially competing claims of connection and community. If people are considerate, they assume that their neighbors are very busy and so try not to intrude on them. Dropping by is no longer neighborly. It is simply rude. We now know why good fences make good neighbors. No one wants to insult the neighbors by acting as though there might be enough slack in their frenetic schedules for them to welcome anyone who just happens to stroll through the gate. We all feel nostalgia for those old-fashioned times when dropping by was neighborly. Homage is paid to them in sitcoms, where friends dropping by is still a way of life, but in real life, people hold themselves back. They don't want to seem odd.

When people treat busyness as a virtue, they step back from one another. They hesitate before visiting or calling or inviting someone over. They hesitate, and the moment passes. People are motivated by kindness; they are thinking of their friends (and neighbors, and relatives). They don't want to be an additional burden, a time sink, when time is already in such short supply. In the short run, they may be right. People may be grateful if others don't bother them, letting them attend to all their work and chores and even their self-improvement projects. Or, more likely, they will start to assume that no one is thinking about them at all. They will start to drift away. They too will stop visiting and calling. We risk becoming a nation in which everyone feels a little neglected, a little left out. And we will all feel that is has been done *to* us, not *by* us.

To buck the trend, people may need a special kind of permission. A friend of ours, who still believes that being neighborly means visiting people, found a solution for herself. Active in her Jewish congregation, she joined the *bikur cholim* committee, a group that offers visits to the sick and homebound. She now visits at least some friends and neighbors with the blessings of a higher authority. Evangelical churches have also been at least partly successful in countering the drift away from a sense of community by refusing to defer to the busyness of modern life and the corresponding importance of not bothering people. These solutions themselves make clear the remarkable power of the emerging taboo against bothering busy neighbors. We must invoke the authority of God to violate it.

When people treat busyness as both a virtue and a sign of success, they want others to see them as virtuously and successfully busy. That can become another reason for stepping back. Good fences also make good neighbors because they can hide an unfashionable lack of busyness. They keep neighbors from seeing that some of us are neither as busy nor as important as we'd like others to believe. We all feel that we will be more respected if we *seem* frightfully busy, so some people create façades of busyness and gradually work themselves into positions where they are *actually* left out.

Consider the small decisions of one shy but delightful young man whom we will call Josh. He had relatives and acquaintances in town who frequently tried to include him in their social gatherings. When Josh received an invitation, he postponed replying. He was not sure he'd be in the mood for a gathering. He was not sure the people would be his kind of crowd. By the time he finished ruminating about an invitation, it was usually too late (at least as Josh saw it) to RSVP at all. So he stayed home and tried to avoid thinking of these people in order not to feel guilty about his procrastination. To keep from thinking, he watched TV, checked his e-mail, and kept track of new bands (he plays the guitar). Needless to say, Josh began to receive very few invitations. People felt he was blowing them off, maybe because he was too busy, maybe because he did not like them.

So Josh came to therapy sessions and regularly complained that he had had a disconnected, lonely weekend in which he slept too much, watched too much TV, and ended up disgusted with himself. What emerged in therapy was that Josh's life was so empty because he didn't want anyone to know that he had so little to do. He avoided social situations because he did not want anyone to ask him what he was doing. The reason: he had a nine-to-five job that did not interest him. The kind of crowd he was afraid to face were friends and relatives who were passionate about what they did, who boasted about their sixty-hour workweeks, who were busy all the time. Josh had made his life emptier because it was not busy enough to feel like a high-status life. When relatives and friends who hadn't given up on him pressed him about why he hadn't shown up to a particular social event, his usual excuse was that he was just too busy.

Josh's procrastination also reflected the dream of an unconstrained life. He was not sure that, when the time came to show up, he would be in the mood. He wanted to keep his options open. Many young people are clear that they don't want to live a life constrained by too many obligations, but deciding which obligations matter the most can leave them indecisive and ambivalent. (The same aspirations often resurface in older people as they begin to dream of retirement; the middle years tend to be the time of simply shouldering the burdens.) When people ignore their moral compass on the topic of social obligations, pretty soon it is hard to make any decision without rumination and hesitation. And busyness both makes it harder to show up and provides convenient cover for not doing so. As one young woman put it, "If I returned every phone call I got in a timely fashion, I'd never have any time for anything else." When the phone calls stop coming, the next small step is to say to oneself something like *Oh, well! I would have been too busy to spend time with them anyway.* The busyness then becomes a camouflage for hurt feelings. But as camouflage, it may work far too well, fooling everyone, including ourselves. Our friends and relations think we are too busy to see them, and new friends give up on us because we seem so unavailable. Josh once admitted that he wished he had a girlfriend who would make him RSVP in a timely way, but it is hard to meet women when you don't socialize very much.

A Social Calendar Is No One's Job

Josh hoped that a girlfriend would be his social secretary. It was not a very realistic hope. The social calendar is no longer anyone's job, unless of course it can be relabeled as networking and shifted into the category of productive busyness. In dual-earner families, neither parent has the time or energy to schedule social events in the way that a 1950s homemaker mother once did. Single people, who would seem to have much more free time than couples with children, have their own obstacles. They need to worry constantly about scheduling social contacts because they have no partners in their homes to do things with spontaneously, but if they call others too much, they bump into the problem of intruding on their friends' busyness. And it is always easy to feel that we are calling others more than they are calling us because the effort of calling is so much more noticeable than the pleasure of receiving a call.

We treat socializing as if it's a frivolous diversion from the tasks at hand rather than an activity that is essential to our well-being as individuals and as a community. It is not just the philosophy of rugged individualism that gets people into trouble (an argument we will confront in the next chapter). It is the notion that time spent socializing for pleasure is not constructive and might, in fact, be time wasted. In many circles these days, working out at the gym is not just acceptable, it's de rigueur. Time watching a movie at home is the new alternative to reading a book. Even combing the Internet for information and bargains can be seen as potentially productive. But hanging out with a friend takes so much time and is so much trouble to set up. And besides, if a person does take the time, he doesn't reliably get credit for it and may even lose a little social status for trying. People might think that he has too much unproductive time on his hands. He might turn into one of those out-of-step people who just drop in on neighbors.

Busyness and Irritability

During a particularly hectic time in our family's life, we considered adopting a family motto—Frantic without a Peep. We were then a family of four. The two parents were busy with psychiatric practices and teaching (and parenting). Our children were the kind who are sometimes described as well-rounded, which really meant that they did a little bit of everything. Our lives demanded a huge amount of logistical planning, a thankless task that fell, as it does in many families, squarely on the mother. Nagging was naturally an essential tool for getting the job done. The nagging was not happily received (or happily offered), but it was the tenuous lifeline that kept everyone from falling off the track on a daily basis.

Each of us wanted to do all that he or she had promised to do, but all those promises created impossible situations. Each of us would be torn in two or three separate directions on a regular basis, probably at least once a week. As parents, we tried sermonizing about the importance of setting priorities and not having too much fun when there was work to be done, but occasionally even we lost the stomach for this kind of talk. We all spent much of our time juggling more than we could manage, but none of us wanted to be a complainer (or at least, none of us wanted to be labeled a complainer). Frantic without a Peep was just the ticket. We all might be frantic, but we would each bear it bravely and quietly.

The problem of course is that Frantic without a Peep doesn't work. "Peeps" continued to happen. We would all get irritable and hypersensitive. During the worst of times, everyone would retreat to his or her workspace or room, and there was little contact within the family. We were just burned out by our collective frenetic pace. As parents, we felt a sense of sadness that family life could sometimes be so lonely, but there seemed to be few solutions. Truthfully, there was a lot of work to be done by each one of us. Or perhaps more truthfully, we were just a little too focused on getting things done, sacrificing a little too much of our comfort with one another for the sake of our separate and collective productivity. We were feeling a little too virtuous about our busyness when we should have been paying attention to some other values.

We think that our family's Frantic without a Peep phase is a microcosm of too much of America at present. Put all of this busyness together—our real busyness, our wish to be seen as busy, our assumption that everyone around us is busy—and it is easy to stop trying and go sulk in our own rooms. Soon our not bothering to call people (or even e-mail them) gets read by others as a sign that we are too caught up in the busy sweep of our own lives to have time for them or to care whether we have time for them. Our friends are not surprised. Our relatives may be indignant, but even they know how hard it is. Most of them also feel too busy and worry about their own productivity and where they stand in the competitive fray. An unspoken understanding develops. It's too bad that we've lost touch, but that's just the way it is.

Necessary Busyness

We do not mean to ignore economic necessity as an important reason for long work hours. We understand that not all busyness is discretionary busyness. Sometimes there is just no choice. Sometimes simply getting by requires two jobs, extra shifts, the sacrifice of almost all free time to work. Barbara Ehrenreich followed her description of the cult of busyness in her book *The Worst Years of Our Lives* with *Nickel and Dimed: On (Not) Getting By in America*, about her failed efforts to get by in a series of minimum-wage jobs that left her exhausted, demoralized, and angry. In *The Two-Income Trap: Why Middle-Class Mothers and Fathers Are Going Broke*, Elizabeth Warren and Amelia Warren Tyagi (a mother-daughter team) use economic data to argue that middle-class working families *require* two incomes to support the basic expenses that in the 1950s could be covered by a father's paycheck alone. Years ago, Mississippi John Hurt sang that the only reason to keep on working is to drive the wolf from the door. The wolf is still at the door of many Americans, and just keeping it at bay can be a cause of social isolation, along with causing a host of other ills. But when the wolf is nowhere in sight, the cult of busyness takes over and the pace does not let up. What changes is that the pace is miraculously transformed from a sign of oppression to a sign of status.

Pacing and Overstimulation

Recently, a patient told us that the day before he had received 160 e-mails that required responses ("Some only needed a few words," he added reassuringly). Like so many people telling busy stories, Carl was bragging more than he was complaining. "A friend of mine says we're *bursters*; we work in bursts." Of course he works in bursts. How else could he survive? It is tempting to add that he is in treatment for severe anxiety and abuse of antianxiety medication. That would be a little simplistic for an explanation, but work-related stress has certainly made both of his problems much worse. The pace is too fast. Carl is constantly being bombarded by simultaneous competing demands on his time and attention. So he alternates between frenetic intensity and medication-induced calm. It is his particular version of a rhythm of life that is increasingly familiar to most of us. We throw ourselves into the fray, proudly battling the demands on us, even asking for more, until we've had it and step back out of the fray—drink or take pills, drive to a New Hampshire farmhouse, or just flop. There seems to be no way to modulate the pace, so people pace themselves with an on-off switch.

Around Christmastime in the 1950s, the U.S. Post Office delivered mail to homes twice a day instead of once a day. One of us remembers the extra excitement that the extra mail deliveries brought with them. The season was brief and it was delightful. But e-mail is like getting two dozen mail deliveries a day, and most of them require a response. They represent work and social demands. (So did the extra deliveries of Christmas cards—*Oh dear, we forgot to send a card to the Fredriksens!*—but as we said, the season was brief.) Add in BlackBerries and beepers and the service economy's invention of the phrase *twenty-four/seven*, and the only way to take a breath is to shut down all the connections, to break contact. It sounds like a bold move, but these days it creates remarkably little commotion. Friends and neighbors no longer make much of it if someone sinks from view for weeks at a time. They assume the person is traveling or involved in a hard project at work or simply needs a break. There is no social stigma, no danger of people wondering why someone has become an eccentric hermit.

Most people understand that we all need breaks from overstimulating lives and give us permission to step back. The only downside of that empathetic understanding is that somewhere in the process of de-stressing by stepping away, a person can start to feel lonely or left out. Friends' understanding that a person sometimes needs to disappear silences an early-warning system that used to be there. When someone disappeared for a few weeks, there would be calls and visits and questions. Now friends are understanding, so there's no early-warning system for people who are in danger of slipping out of their social worlds and drifting off

so far that a temporary disconnection becomes permanent—
a problem made worse because people can so easily start to feel left
out and embarrassed by their loneliness. In chapter 4, we will look
closely at the experience of feeling left out, an experience that
plays a central role in much of human history and current affairs
even though the words *left out* sound small and childish. The consequences of feeling left out are both surprising and profound,
making it almost impossible to imagine a graceful reentry into the
comforts of connection.

Pacing and Values

"God helps those who help themselves." "Idle hands are the
Devil's playground." Whether we quote these maxims very often
or not at all, their spirit has shaped our country. The cult of busyness may be fueled by current customs and technology, but it rests
on three sturdy pillars of American life: Calvinism, capitalism, and
competitiveness. From Calvinism comes faith that God is smiling
on those who achieve material success. From capitalism comes a
perpetual hope (realized often enough) that hard work and new
ideas will be rewarded. From a reverence for the competitive spirit
comes a genuine admiration for winners. These three intertwined
ideas have helped create previously unimagined prosperity. They
also invite us to try harder, to work longer, to give back (collec-
tively) hundreds of millions of vacation hours each year, to treat
each and every day as another day to succeed. They teach us not
to peep when life feels too frantic, or at least to peep softly. A loud
complaint might alert others to our difficulties and our failures
and suggest that we are not among God's Elect.

These same ideas encourage us to elevate self-improvement to
a religion and an art form. In a curious twist that no eighteenth-
century Calvinist could have anticipated, cultivation of the body is
now evidence of being among the Elect, being a winner. Our age
places extraordinary emphasis on health and exercise. Well-to-do

adults in their twenties and thirties try to make time in a busy week for regular workouts and healthy eating, with relationships often playing second fiddle to the care of the self. Obesity has acquired a new socioeconomic dimension, being more prevalent now in the poor than in the rich, a curious reversal of ancient associations. Many young adults cannot understand how their parents' generation survived without time for themselves, which often is code for exercise. Recently, we were invited to speak to a group of young woman doctors about balancing work and family life. One of them asked how much time Jacqueline used to put aside for workouts while she juggled being the mother of young children and being a doctor. The simple answer was "none." There was a moment of generational bewilderment. Eyes widened with surprise.

These same three ideas do a wonderful job of fueling a consumer-driven economy. They transform shopping from a chore to an opportunity to prove that we are winners. "Whoever dies with the most toys wins." People don't really believe that. Or do they? Every daily activity becomes a sprint for the gold, and no one wants to be left at the starting line.

The mix of Calvinist roots, capitalism, and competitiveness also teaches us not to be held back by inconvenient bonds that might slow us down. In recent years, a new set of maxims has emerged: "You have to love yourself before you can love someone else," "To live with others, you must first master the art of living alone." Burger King stripped it down to the bone with its long-lived slogan "Have it your way!" Our lives are in our own hands, shaped by our energy and our gumption, free from compromise, dependence, and obligation. In the microcosm of fast food, Burger King offers every American a taste of the uncompromised life. There are nobler visions of the uncompromised life with deep roots in American thought, American mythology, and American values. If busyness provides the push that moves us away from social connectedness, those visions provide the pull, which will be the subject of our next chapter.

So what happened to some other classic American traits, such as friendliness, openness, charity, sharing, and neighborliness? Tocqueville described America as a country of associations. If Americans saw something that needed fixing, they formed an association to tackle the problem. Have these ever-so-American traits gone underground, or are they flourishing only in Lake Wobegon, as Garrison Keillor would like us to believe? Many of these traits have historically been nurtured by organized religious communities. As more people moved their spirituality away from institutions and toward a more private experience (the religious equivalent of having it your way), the group pressures and encouragement that nurtured these values have waned. It is impressive how much it matters when a peer group, such as the members of a congregation, compete to see who can do the most good. When competition is focused on who can eat the healthiest food or who can spend the most workout time at the gym, instead of on who can do the most good for others, much of the impetus toward charity, friendliness, and sharing is lost. (Although not all; there are important countertrends, including a dramatic rise in community service and the creation of nonprofit organizations, that we will address in the final chapter.)

What we are left with is a persistently frantic state of busyness. Since everyone else looks frantic too, we don't see why we personally should be uncomfortable with it. Our only peeps or complaints might be to the therapists whom we have hired, because at least they will not tell anyone else about our discomfort. Our small steps back from the fray have left us in our dens of technological connectedness feeling curiously lonely. And even though we have arranged many things about our lives to be just the way we supposedly like them, our overall sense of contentment seems to be going down. Even worse, when we arrange our lives to suit our own special needs and try to have it our way, it is easy to lose the habits of sharing and taking the common good into consideration. As the sociologists who wrote the 1986 book *Habits of the Heart* told us, a person is subject to a malaise if he or she does nothing to contribute to the common good. Both the busyness of our lives and our efforts to escape from the busyness of our lives threaten our connections to one another. Both the busyness and the escapes discourage us from taking others into consideration. On a small scale, we as individuals may be seen as a bit selfish by our elders, who remember when giving back was the way to win the respect from friends and colleagues. On a larger scale, we as a people lose the respect of the world if we are citizens of a country that doesn't think about others while it uses up the world's nonsustainable resources.

Both individuals and groups get set in their ways. The more isolated the individuals or groups are, the more set in their ways they become. People lose the limber agility to adapt that comes from dealing with the adjustments, conflicts, and compromise required when living with others. The end result is that each person's efforts get funneled into having things exactly his or her own way, rather than into exploring the happiness and contentment that might derive from working toward what is best for a larger group. In *Collapse*, Jared Diamond argues that societies that have become extinct usually had a situational or cultural blindness that led them to run themselves into the ground. If we continue in the direction we our headed, our society's epitaph might be "They had it their way."

CHAPTER 3

Self-Reliance

Do Lonesome Cowboys Sing the Blues?

In "Self-Reliance," Ralph Waldo Emerson wrote, "There is a time in every man's education when he arrives at the conviction...that though the wide universe is full of good, no kernel of nourishing corn can come to him but through his toil bestowed on that plot of ground which is given to him to till."[1]

Not many Americans survive on their own corn these days. A patient recently told us her father's story. Finishing college in the late 1960s, he read a book called *Five Acres and Independence*, went for ten acres, and set about raising a small family while completely "living off the land." Her smile expressed affection, admiration, and a gentle sense of the absurdity of her father's quest. The mirroring smiles of her listeners reminded us that his quest touched something deep within all of us—a shared belief in the transcendence of a life nourished by corn raised with one's own hands on his own land. That vision remains resonant, barely diminished by the facts of our lives or the wisdom of economists. By comparison, an interdependent life appears unmanly, unheroic, and un-American. "Society everywhere is in conspiracy against the manhood of every one of its members," cries Emerson, and his cry resounds to this day.

Good Lord, you say, *it's another diatribe against American individ-*

ualism. Hasn't that ground been worked over enough times already? We believe we can add something new to the familiar arguments about the virtues and vices of self-reliance. We hope to develop an understanding of the interaction between grand cultural ideals and the small choices that individuals make while just trying to get through the day. It is an interaction that our work with patients brings into particularly clear focus, since the main business of psychotherapy is to tease out the connections between underlying assumptions (which are often unnoticed or unconscious) and the particular paths (or sometimes dead ends) that a person travels down.

As we saw in the preceding chapter, the frenetic pace of everyday life pushes people toward greater isolation for relief and escape. That push would not be nearly as effective, however, if there were not a pull as well. The pull is a very seductive picture of standing apart as a victory, not a retreat. Ever since Ralph Waldo Emerson wrote his famous essay and Henry David Thoreau set out to embody the concept in his cabin on Walden Pond, a long series of American icons have idealized the concept of self-reliance. Emerson's essay helped define self-reliance as the quintessential American virtue for generations of high-school students. The image of Thoreau's contemplative solitude, immersed more in nature than human society, added romance to virtue. But Emerson and Thoreau were working with already-resonant images. The living-off-the-land quote from Emerson that begins this chapter was a metaphor—his subject was intellectual, not nutritional, self-reliance—but he chose a metaphor that was presumably just as evocative in his day as it is in ours. To depend on others for what we need makes us uncomfortable and confounds our reverence for self-reliance. Thoreau wisely chose not to report in his writings on Walden Pond that the luxury of his contemplation was made possible in part by his family's successful pencil factory. That mundane fact undercuts only his myth, however, not the wisdom of his writings. Self-reliance *is* a virtue. It's just a complicated virtue. When treated as a sufficient goal in itself, it can lead to a life, a country, and a planet out of balance. Small choices at the margins of busy lives accumulate and result in people feeling left out, ashamed, and sometimes very angry.

The ideal of the outsider—an individual who stands apart from a community yet is connected enough to affect its destiny, or maybe even to save it—exerts a powerful pull, shaping the stories we want to tell about ourselves and directing the choices we make in order to live out those stories. Probably all of us can recall early encounters with that ideal. Richard still remembers a grade-school encounter with the life of Daniel Boone. Many facts have faded over the years, but not that image of a man who moved on whenever he could see the smoke from a neighbor's chimney. A boy's daydreams about being that man, even though the boy was growing up in the middle of Manhattan, have not fully faded either.

We are about to make a turn in our argument and a shift in our vocabulary, and we want to make that shift in plain view. There is a slightly darker version of the ideal of self-reliance, one that is likely to be disavowed in public but is no less powerful in our private mythologies. We have already named it: the ideal of the outsider who stands apart yet shapes our country's destiny. It is the same myth, but with the emphasis on apartness rather than self-sufficiency. They are two sides of the same coin. Emerson recognized the kinship in his essay. "These are the voices which we hear in solitude, but they grow faint and inaudible as we enter into the world...Whoso would be a man, must be a nonconformist." A person must be willing to stand apart from the crowd, unattached to "these communities of opinion." In crucial ways, one must bravely steel oneself to be an *outsider*, far from the comforting smoke of a neighbor's chimney. The word *outsider* bears a much more complicated emotional charge than the word *self-reliance*, even though each follows from the other. The idea of being an outsider taps directly into the universal fear (and universal experience) of being left out. The outsider sits, gazing at us, both a national ideal and a childhood nightmare.

Lonesome Heroes

Outsiders are the bedrock of the American heroic landscape. If we begin to forget, we get a regular reminder at least every four years, when we see politicians desperately reworking their life stories to protect themselves from that most damning of labels—the Washington insider. Even in the bitterly divisive politics of recent presidential campaigns, conservatives and liberals remain united in their devotion to a shared heroic ideal. Being connected becomes code for being corrupt. Some of the argument is about privilege: no one wants to be seen as having it easy. The heart of the argument, however, is a profoundly important question. What makes a person strong, wise, and trustworthy? The answer, looping back to Emerson, is self-reliance.

The culture is flooded with countless movies that all give the same answer, as they have for most of the life of the film industry. Characters played by Clint Eastwood and John Wayne, in slightly overlapping generations, have embodied some of the more well-known outsider heroes, to the point that the actors themselves have become iconic. The authors' own list of favorite characters probably has more to do with when we grew up and a certain randomness in our moviegoing habits than with anything else, so we invite readers to consider their own favorite movie heroes and see how often they turn out to be outsiders. We also turned to an expert, Jamie Delson, an old friend, movie buff, and former critic who (we discovered) once watched about fifteen hundred Westerns in one year. We asked him for good examples of the idealized loner/outsider who gets the job done and saves the community but is not entirely part of the community. He listed several specific movies (*Shane, Dirty Harry, Rio Bravo, The Man Who Shot Lib-*

erty Valence), but the most interesting part of his response was "any 1930s/1940s B Western." This is a category filled with an astonishing number of movies, movies that both reflected and reshaped the country's collective self-image. Through their cultural offspring, which are also numerous, they continue to affect us today.[2]

Rio Bravo, a 1959 Western in which John Wayne, Dean Martin, and Ricky Nelson take a brave and lonely stand, is particularly interesting because it was an explicit effort to correct earlier myths. In a 1962 interview with Peter Bogdanovich, the director Howard Hawks explained how he came to make the movie: "It started with some scenes in a picture called *High Noon*, in which Gary Cooper ran around trying to get help and no one would give him any. And that's rather a silly thing for a man to do, especially since at the end of the picture he is able to do the job by himself."[3] Or, as Hawks put it in a later interview, "I didn't think a good sheriff was going to go running around town like a chicken with his head off asking for help."[4] Most of us remember Gary Cooper in *High Noon* as a brave man standing alone. Hawks tells us that even he was not self-reliant enough to be a real American hero. He looked for help.

Ben Franklin said it best in *Poor Richard's Almanack:* "God helps those who help themselves." Hawks shapes Franklin's epigram into an effective parable and a great Western. The sociologist Robert Bellah locates its fundamental source in our country's primarily Protestant culture, specifically "the near exclusive focus on the relation between Jesus and the individual, where accepting Jesus Christ as one's personal Lord and Savior becomes almost the whole of piety." Bellah goes on:

> If I may trace the downward spiral of this particular Protestant distortion, let me say that it begins with the statement "If I'm all right with Jesus, then I don't need the church,"

which we hear from some of the people we interviewed for *Habits of the Heart*... Some may think that Jesus-and-me piety is very different from the individual as the preeminent being in the universe, but I am suggesting that they are only a hair apart.[5]

Bellah is developing a critique of American individualism, and we will come back to that. However, for the moment let us stick with the myth, its power to shape what each of us wants to be and its power to help rationalize what each of us inadvertently becomes.

Westerns are an ideal genre for the development of outsider myths because images of lonesome heroes usually emerge from images of the American frontier. As we said in an earlier book about loneliness, America is a country created by tie breakers.

> We need to remind ourselves that the first members of each family to emigrate to America *had* to be "tie breakers." In choosing to embrace the adventure of starting fresh in a brand-new place, they had to be willing to give up the comfort of being known, recognized, and tied into a larger family unit and its surrounding community. The first step of "coming to America" involved practicing individualism in the extreme. As each relative arrived to join an enlarging family group, individualism and courageous independence became less of a requirement. Yet the glorification of those qualities remained an important part of the process of willingly breaking ties, a process recapitulated over and over again throughout our history as Americans moved the frontier farther west. Essentially, the whole country would never have been settled if Americans hadn't idealized concepts like "going your own way" and "forging your own path."[6]

A culture's attitude toward the ties that bind automatically and pervasively shapes how its members see the world and how they see themselves. It even restricts the thoughts that they can imagine themselves thinking. These cultural blinders are made clear by our favorite question in cross-cultural research. People are asked to complete the sentence "I love my mother but..."[7] In Western countries, the usual response is critical and distancing, something along the lines of "I love my mother... but she's just so difficult," with the details readily provided. In Southeast Asia, the usual response is not criticism but appreciation. "I love my mother... I can never repay all that she has done for me." What makes the exercise so powerful is that most people (including the authors) cannot imagine the other form of response until they are presented with it. It simply does not exist as a possible way of thinking. As Americans, we are automatically prepared to question the value of our strongest bonds and to step away from them when necessary, relying instead on ourselves. The advantages of that attitude in our history are clear, as are its risks.

The American frontier has also given us feminine versions of self-reliance and apartness, like Laura Ingalls Wilder's classic stories *Little House in the Big Woods* and *Little House on the Prairie*. The titles themselves evoke our pioneers' isolation in the vast uncivilized spaces of the frontier. They also suggest how the feminine ideal differs from the masculine one. The frontiersman is alone, surrounded by nature. The frontierswoman is at the hearth, holding together a family—which is itself alone, surrounded by nature. The emphasis shifts from the self-reliant individual to the self-reliant family (which may be making it without the presence of an adult male). Those dreams are picked up today by magazines, such as *Better Homes and Gardens* and *Real Simple*, that show their readers how to create homes with the feel of a little house in the big woods, every room bearing witness to the industry of the homemaker's own hands.

We can make too much of the gender-specificity of these ideals, however. As we grow up, we each draw inspiration and hope from real-life and storied figures on both sides of the gender divide, even if most of us try to shape the result into something that conforms to conventional cultural ideas of masculine and feminine. Heroic fathers, real and imagined, inspire daughters, and heroic mothers, real and imagined, inspire sons. One of the most determinedly self-reliant individuals we know is a female professor who simply will not ask for help from colleagues, friends, or family, even on joint projects where others are not doing their share. She would rather do it herself, even when the "it" is someone else's job, than "run around town...asking for help." She is perpetually overextended and regularly exhausted, but Howard Hawks would approve of her.

Similarly, *Real Simple* may have women as its target audience, but that "little house in the big woods" feel has the same fascination for men. There is a remarkable passage in Charles Reich's 1970 celebration of "the coming American revolution" *The Greening of America*. Reich offers a hymn of praise to jeans and the way they wrinkle and mold themselves to reveal the individuality of the wearer's body, in contrast to the obliteration of individuality by the neatly pressed corporate suit.[8] The passage is over the top but not entirely off the mark. Reich thought he was witnessing a revolution. Instead, he was watching an extreme version of a generational cycle: the young keep rediscovering American individualism as though it were their own new idea. Jeans carried that message well (at least in the sixties) not only because they were unpressed and unstarched, but also because they stirred up deep in their wearers' psyches the whole mystique of the American frontier and the rugged loners who populated it (at least in our imagination)—cowboys, prospectors, sheriffs, all those outsider-hero types. We speak from personal knowledge, coming of age in the sixties ourselves. Richard remembers getting his first pair of blue jeans when he was a small boy, just before he went off to summer camp "in the big woods." The excitement he felt was not about a premonition of counterculture and rebellion. It was about cowboys.

A Spoonful of Sugar

Now we may seem to have wandered very far from the causes of social isolation, but the cultural myths and heroes that people grew up with are never very far away. They shape their hopes and fears. Sometimes their effects are direct and obvious, like the father setting off with his young family, book in hand, to live off the land. Sometimes the spotlight shines right on them, like a 2007 *New York Times* report on a $200,000 NASA prize to design a new space glove:

> Americans, perhaps more so than people of other nations, have great faith in the idea of the outsider inventor. The stories of inventors who made it out of their garages (Steve Jobs) and those who stayed there (Philo T. Farnsworth) are part of the national mythology...Americans seem drawn to the story of the outsider-made-good with an intensity that has riveted the nation from the earliest amateur contests featured regularly in vaudeville to the latest version of such shows, like *American Idol*. In America, the self-made citizen is a kind of superhero.[9]

Sometimes the tone is facetious, as in the portrait of a Montana prosecutor in *Profiles in Courage for Our Time*, a collection of essays edited by Caroline Kennedy. The story begins with a classic image: "A band of isolated settlers among whom is a quiet, solitary man, a loner, who stands tall for justice."[10] The tone is tongue-in-cheek but the Montana prosecutor really is a hero, and the reverence beneath the irony is clear. The same grudging respect for American ideals is clear in a column by David Brooks mocking a current crop of tough-women song lyrics: "When Americans face something that's psychologically traumatic, they invent an autonomous Lone Ranger fantasy hero who can deal with it."[11]

More often, outsider-hero myths operate in the background, just out of view, making people uneasy when they fall short. Advertisers get it, selling the costumes people need to quiet that uneasiness. The *Sundance* catalog, spun off from the film festival, shows beautiful women wearing Western-style clothes under the words *independent, in film and attire*. Most of the cars and trucks sold in the United States are first sighted in ads showing a single vehicle traveling alone through the same country that appeared in our favorite Westerns. We know what real Americans were meant to be, we know that we have strayed, but we can buy consolation and illusion.

We also fool ourselves more directly. Politicians are not the only ones who make patently false claims that they are outsiders. In the recently published *The Accidental Investment Banker*, an account of ten years on the job, Jonathan Knee says that "although I liked to think of myself as the consummate outsider I had, over time, quietly adopted the values of the industry of which I had been a part."[12] What is remarkable here is not that a man comes to adopt the values of a job that pays him lavishly, but that a man who arrived at that job by way of Yale and Stanford could still see himself as the *consummate outsider*. It's a wonderful phrase. The fear of being left out is so basic that many people recoil at first from the word *outsider*, but Knee captures the shine and status that's attached to being an outsider if it's done right.

As a nation, we work hard to burnish that shine and then claim it as our own. As psychiatrists, we are no longer surprised when patients who are perceived as consummate *insiders* tell us that they have always felt like outsiders and misfits. It is hard to give examples without betraying confidentiality, since their insider credentials usually come from the prominence of their families or their work, but even when the claim looks most absurd, it is usually deeply felt. No amount of privilege lets anyone make it to adulthood without having had powerful experiences of being left out. One of our children's teachers in grade school once asked the Zen-like question "Are all potatoes alike?" He was trying to teach about diversity. The answer (we think) is that it depends on whether you focus on the similarities or the differences. Almost everyone can draw on memories of feeling *in* and memories of feeling *out*. The claim to outsider status is made through a shift in emphasis rather than by an outright lie. The point for our current argument is that the claim is not just a confession of pain or embarrassment (although that is often a part of it). The claim is made with pride, a statement of strength and courage. It is the pride of living up to the ideal of the outsider hero.

It is also a neat psychological trick. By standing tall in one's own mind, side by side with heroes, each of us is suddenly no longer alone but part of a group. It may be a group of outsiders, but the individual is proud to belong and (just as important) is comforted by belonging. That magical transformation is the historic miracle of America that is inscribed on the Statue of Liberty:

> Give me your tired, your poor,
> Your huddled masses yearning to breathe free,
> The wretched refuse of your teeming shore.
> Send these, the homeless, tempest-tost to me,
> I lift my lamp beside the golden door.

The promise is that a great nation will be created by those who have been left out. When we conjure up our American pantheon of outsiders, we work the same magic in our own minds to comfort ourselves as we drift apart.

That psychological magic becomes the spoonful of sugar that makes painful experiences of being left out easier to swallow. That pride is a partial answer to a mystery that emerges from the preceding chapter. Since we leave ourselves out without entirely meaning to, why don't we just take the obvious corrective action and get ourselves reconnected? One piece of the answer is that we end up in a place that looks a lot like where we always knew that we were supposed to stand.

Childhood Demons

It is also the last place on earth that a person would want to be. Last year, we tried out some of our ideas on two old friends. "No one wants to feel like an outsider!" was their impassioned response. The sociologist in the couple explained that in his field the word *outsider* meant what psychiatrists might call an antisocial personality—bad guys, not good guys. The schoolteacher in the couple talked about how devastating it was for a child to feel like an outsider and how that child's desperate parents would march into school to demand that teachers protect their child from ever being treated like one. Of course, our friends were right. It feels terrible to be treated like an outsider. No one likes to be left out. Even B Westerns derive a certain emotional power from a simple truth—to stand alone one must vanquish those familiar demons.

Man is a social animal. That commonplace observation is true at the most basic level. Our biological survival depends on our attachments, and our capacity for attachment is built into our biology. And not just our capacity for attachment but our longing for it. How could it be otherwise? The biology of attachment is just beginning to be understood (with the neuropeptides oxytocin and vasopressin currently playing starring roles), but scientists knew it had to be there. No species is long for this world if its biology does not drive it to seek what it needs for its survival. The outsider is heroic partly because he or she has conquered a desire that holds most of the rest of us in its sway. We train our children to battle that desire from an early age, to enjoy having their own rooms, their own belongings, their particular preferences in food and in style. Many a middle-class child arrives at college to discover that sharing a room with another student is extremely stressful after a youth spent learning the joys of *not* sharing, of keeping attachments loose and fluid.

In the next chapter, we will take up the biology of attachment as science. It is an exciting and emerging story. The part of the story we will tell now is the lived experience of that biology. No one is lucky enough to grow up without feeling left out some of the time. And however well or poorly we deal with the wounds, feeling left out cuts us deeply. Most parents and preschool teachers and former children can conjure up scenes of tears suddenly erupting in a group of children. If you want to bet on the cause, the odds-on favorite is a shift in the group that has left someone out. Richard remembers being in elementary school and coming in from recess with one cheek bleeding, scratched by the nails of another boy lashing out in desperate anger. It is a terribly embarrassing memory. A group of boys had suddenly gelled and was taunting another boy, who was in that moment an outsider, for reasons long lost to memory (if they were ever clear at all). Richard joined in with the tormenters (on this part he is clear) simply because he wanted to belong to the group.

Feeling left out or included is one of the great engines of human emotion and human affairs, whether at the level of individuals, groups, or nations. Sigmund Freud came very close to understanding its importance, but he was distracted by sex. He described the now famous Oedipal conflict as *the* crucial moment in a boy's development. Briefly stated, the conflict arises alongside the young boy's dawning awareness that his parents have a sexual relationship with each other that excludes him. Freud chose to emphasize the sexual part of the story. (In a wonderfully disarming letter, he wrote, "The connection between obsessional neurosis and sexuality is not always so obvious...If anyone less mono-ideistic than I am had looked for it, he would have over-looked it."[13]) That same dawning awareness remains an incredibly powerful and disruptive idea for a child (of either gender) even when the word *sexual* is left out. A child's world is changed forever by the recognition that his or her parents have a connection with each other that sometimes leaves the child out. What a transforming idea that is, particularly as it slowly ripples out and colors the wider world: *There are connections, powerful connections, between other people that leave me out! Out in the cold where it's dangerous to be on my own. This is sure not the place where I want to be.*

A patient who is a successful artist and an attractive woman was talking about her plans to attend a gallery opening in New York City. She had a new jacket that she wanted to wear, but it was red and this was the New York art scene. Everyone would be wearing black. She confronted her insecurities. She reminded herself of the long tradition of defiant individualism in her own family. She buttressed her determination with a pep talk about the importance and even the status of artists who march to their own drummers. She marched off triumphantly and wore her red jacket to the opening. She returned mortified. It had been horrible. She was so embarrassed. Everyone else really had been dressed in black. She felt like a hick from Boston, a misfit who stood out like a sore thumb. She would never be that stupid again. Black it would be.

She had had every reason for confidence. She knew better, but the experience of people seeming to be connected to one another in ways that left her out touched something in her, something that is hidden away in all of us, and it made the gallery opening unbearable in red. And memories began to pour out, memories of feeling different and insecure in her boarding school, of not quite belonging in the cool kids' group, and, yes, even sexual memories of her divorced mother's locked door behind which was a series of lovers. Being left out in the cold is a terrible feeling, even for an artist.[14]

An Artist Responds

Our friend Pete, who is also an artist, reminds us to maintain a crucial balance in our critique of lonesome heroes. After all, they *do* save the town. And, in a small way, our patient's decision to put aside her red jacket the next time she attends an opening in New York is a capitulation to a petty tyranny of the majority. Pete himself has long wrestled with the issues we examine in this book. For nearly thirty years, he has mitigated the forced solitude his work imposes by staying seriously involved in his community's politics, municipal finances, and education. He recognizes that the excessive isolation of his work can lead to an unhealthy self-absorption, but he is rightly proud of his individualism even when he engages with his community. The history of social progress in this nation has often been marked by individuals who risked the disapproval of their communities in the name of higher goals. Pete offers a list off the top of his head: white Southern editors who spoke out early against Jim Crow laws; cops who risk careers and more by exposing corruption in their departments; muckraking journalists, academics, writers, and social reformers of all stripes who expose fraud, venality, and exploitation; young couples who defy family and community expectations to marry across ethnic, religious, or class boundaries.

The dark side of community can be complacency, cowardice, and complicity. A healthy community, whether it appreciates the fact or not, needs both the bonds of loyalty and the willingness to risk isolation and loneliness in the name of a greater good. Both

individuals and communities thrive when they can hold on to
the tension between belonging and standing alone. We need to be
limber—to be able to step away and step toward—but it is surprisingly easy to get stuck.

One More Twist: The Myth of the Insider

So whether it is the result of taking small steps back from frantic
daily lives or simply of the inevitable jolts of social situations in
which other folks look better connected, people keep colliding
with the old familiar feelings of being left out. Once again we ask,
"Why don't most people efficiently fix the problem and just reconnect?" We have given a partial answer—they reach instead for
stories that make them more comfortable and even proud of being
left out and thus act as an antidote to the feelings of shame that being excluded stirs up. The rest of the answer will seem a bit odd.
The same struggles that lead people to idealize notions about outsiders also invite them to idealize the *insiders*.

We all know who the insiders are. We have all envied them
as we go about our own personal quests or even as we are just trying our best to get by, our shoulders pushing against that damned
heavy wheel. They are the ones who have it easy—because of accidents of birth and family and unearned privilege, because of who
they know and who looks out for them. A simple example is that
coterie of New York City artists at the opening, the little group
who all knew what to wear and how to behave and what the hot
topics were and whose work was in, the ones who had all the right
connections with all the right gallery owners and museum curators
and cut everyone else out of the chance for an opening of her own.
That at least is a version of the story that our patient told on her
return from the Big City, having been shamed and enraged by her
obvious (red) badge of her outsider status. Each job, each career,
each area of human striving has some version of that story—the
one who got the job or the promotion or the chance to perform

because he or she comes from the right family or went to the right school or belongs to the right club.

In the same way we let our imaginations run free about outsiders on the open range, we also imagine the pleasures of those in the opposite situation. We imagine how lucky the insiders must be, with all those connections that smooth their way and make their rise to wealth and power so easy. We imagine people who are used to getting everything without the solitary hard work that we ourselves need to devote to our dreams if we are to get anything at all to work out. We imagine people who are just more talented than we are, endowed with better genes that let them soar to the top while we continue to struggle. Soon our imaginations have populated America with lots of insiders who are leaving us out. We all try to persuade ourselves that we don't really mind feeling disconnected, that we are proud to stand apart and will make it anyway. But if this effort at denial fails, we begin to feel mistrustful and a bit sorry for ourselves. Pride begins to give way to bitterness, and another vicious cycle starts to power up.

A simple example comes from another patient. She teaches at a local elementary school and is clearly extraordinarily good at her demanding job and very well respected. Yet she came in one day in the middle of a dramatic downward spiral of depression and had suicide on her mind. She talked about feeling completely left out at work, discarded, maybe on the verge of being fired. She was in the middle of a divorce, so being left out was particularly frightening and she really needed her job at that point, but her work had always been an oasis of competence and inclusion. We began to look at the evidence that she was being left out at school. She was not invited to an old-timers' lunch with a cohort of teachers who were about the same age as her but had all been hired together, long before she'd started at the school. The principal had not asked her to serve on a particular committee even though she'd asked everyone else our patient worked with to serve on it.

The principal was new and young, and thus, our patient thought, she probably wanted teachers like herself, with fresh ideas and boundless energy. Our patient felt left out by everyone, so she withdrew into her office, closed the door, and began preparing for her lonely exit from a job that she loved. She did not belong in either club at work, neither the old-timers nor the youngsters. It was just a matter of time before she was squeezed out of her job.

As she listened to her own argument, it began to fall apart in her hands. She ended up shaking her head, with a rueful smile on her face. After she left the therapy session, she arranged a lunch for her department, talked to her principal (who thought she was doing a great job and had not wanted to overburden her with another committee), and came back the next week in a wonderful mood. Without the change in direction that took place in her therapy session, she would have stepped farther away from others rather than toward them and would have dramatically increased the odds that she would continue to be left out in the future. With that change in direction, she began to find ways to get herself included. Instead of staking a bitter claim as an outsider, she simply found ways to become an insider again.

First Reality Check

But insiders do have it easy! Or at least easier. And in this country there are powerful markers of being an outsider, such as ethnicity, religion, gender, and education, that cannot be fixed by just planning a department lunch. One of the most bubble-bursting news stories in recent years was a study that found Northern Europe and Canada had greater intergenerational economic mobility than the United States.[15] If that study holds up, it will require a stunning revision of our national self-image (and maybe some revision of our national policies). America's most famous self-defining phrase, the Land of Opportunity, has always meant that we see our country as a land where, through hard work and cleverness, outsiders can become insiders. That land still exists, but it is no simple paradise. Not everybody can join every club, and there are certain clubs that do a remarkable job of greasing the wheels for their members. Even the admissions policy of a local garden club was summed up to us with the phrase "It's not what you grow, it's who you know." We don't mean to be naïve about how the world works. We just mean to point out that in individual lives, when dealing with other individuals, there are moments when one can choose between remaining left out and trying gracefully to become included. The trajectories of our lives are shaped by the sum of those small choices. The social fabric of the country is also shaped by the sum of those small choices. Two ideas push a person to take a step back: the heartening idealization of the outsider and the bitter idealization of the insider's easy life.

Second Reality Check

But the outsiders weren't really outside! No one really made it alone, not even on the frontier. The authors had originally called the classic American hero a *not-quite-outsider*. We were trying to evoke an image of someone who stood at the far edge of a community but not completely outside it. *Not-quite-outsider* was just too clumsy to conjure up much of anything for most people, but it remains a more precise description of the ideal than the word *outsider*. Life on the frontier was a complex mix of self-reliance and inescapable interdependence. John Mack Faragher, a historian who wrote about frontier life, described self-sufficiency as a community experience, not something achieved by individuals or separate families: "Cabin raisings, log rollings, hayings, huskings, harvesting or threshing were all traditionally communal affairs...Farm families depended upon their neighbors to supply the variety of goods and tools, and the extra supplies of labor, that made economic life possible."[16] As one settler explained to another, "Your wheelbarrows, your shovels, your utensils of all sorts belong not to yourself but to the public who do not think it necessary even to ask a loan, but take it for granted."[17]

The same spirit of self-sufficiency as a community experience persists on the modern frontier. One of our colleagues spends several months each year on a ranch in Montana and reports the following: "Each summer when the big truck comes by to deliver the hay for the animals, five or six of the able-bodied men in our small town suddenly materialize to help us unload the truck. No one asked them to come. They just knew we would need help with unloading the hay, and they know we'd do the same for them."

Interdependency is easier to swallow when everyone needs help and knows it. When help becomes exclusively paid rather than reciprocal, people forget how important it is. Even though self-sufficiency is usually described as a rural or small-town value, that kind of forgetting is easiest in affluent cities and their suburbs.

Newly arrived immigrants may need to break free of ties to get themselves here, but once they arrive, most immigrants immediately set about reconstructing tightly knit networks of support based on extended families and fellow immigrants from the same town or region in the old country. They value closeness over privacy, if only out of necessity, packing large families into small houses and apartments. Director Barry Levinson's autobiographical 1990 movie *Avalon* does a wonderful job of tracing the transformation of a family over the span of three generations from off-the-boat closeness and dependency to suburban separateness and self-reliance. Heartfelt Netflix postings about the movie demonstrate how directly it captured the family stories of many viewers.

There were true outsiders on the frontier and in the waves of immigrants to this country, outsiders, as sociologists tend to use the term, the misfits who would neither give nor receive help, the kind of person others would never want to share their wheelbarrows or shovels with. At that time, there was certainly more room to hide an unsavory past or make a fresh start. The myth is not that outsiders existed but that they were the reliable heroes and saviors of those sadly unself-reliant wheelbarrow sharers. The problem with the mythic elevation of the outsider to savior is that it makes us proud and complacent when we feel left out and apart. That alchemy is a modern reworking of the idea of self-reliance. As Susan Cheever says in her account of the lives of Emerson, Thoreau, and the rest of the genius cluster in nineteenth-century Concord, Massachusetts, "These people were closer to nature than we can ever be, of necessity—and they depended on friends and neighbors because they had to."[18] Or, in the words of MIT historian Pauline Maier, "Nowadays, our needs being less overt, [they] are easier to deny and so we neglect human needs that earlier Americans readily acknowledged."[19] It is hard to imagine what those earlier Americans would have made of a recent story in the *Boston Globe* in which marketing consultant and author Marian Salzman predicted that over the next few years homes would become "fully equipped compounds that offer both comfort and entertainment—and very little reason to leave."[20]

We must even add a reality check to Howard Hawks's history of his movie *Rio Bravo*. Hawks was engaged in a little bit of mythmaking about his own mythmaking. Remember his account (repeated here in a longer quote):

> It started with some scenes in a picture called *High Noon*, in which Gary Cooper ran around trying to get help and no one would give him any. And that's rather a silly thing for a man to do, especially since at the end of the picture he is able to do the job by himself. So I said, we'll just do the opposite, and take a real professional viewpoint: as Wayne says when he's offered help, "If they're really good, I'll take them. If not, I'll just have to take care of them."

The noted film critic Robin Wood adds: "That's fair enough, as far as it goes, but it contains one inaccuracy (Cooper *does* need help at the end) and one omission: Hawks might have mentioned that Wayne needs help at every critical moment, and gets it."[21]

Our Stubborn Dreams

In 1894, the groundbreaking historian Frederick Jackson Turner delivered a paper titled "The Significance of the Frontier in American History" to the American Historical Association.[22] He argued that the advancing frontier furnished "the forces dominating American character," particularly "that dominant individualism, working for good and for evil." Historians have debated the so-called Turner thesis over the last century. John Mack Faragher's studies of community on the frontier are part of that debate. Whether or not Turner was right about the true nature of life on the frontier and its effect on American character, more than a hundred years later he speaks with uncanny precision about what Americans think our character *should* be. He called the frontier "the outer edge of the wave—the meeting point between savagery and civilization." Contemporary historians may be revising the understanding of frontier life, but they have not yet touched our dreams. Each of us still yearns for a life on that outer edge, the life of the not-quite-outsider, a little connected to others but still bravely, inventively, and defiantly outside.

Turner proclaimed that "the frontier has gone, and with its going has closed the first period of American history." More than a hundred years later, it is not yet gone from our psyches. *Five Acres and Independence* is still selling well on Amazon.com, and a 2003 book called *The Self-Sufficient Life and How to Live It* is selling even better. Those dreams don't lead most people to buy farms, however. Instead, when the twists and turns of life leave us a little disconnected and a little lonely, those dreams lead us to smile quietly (if a bit sadly) to ourselves and tap into our inner resources rather than invite anyone over for dinner. When we run out of sugar, we draw on that brave tradition of life on the outer edge, get in our own cars, and go buy our own boxes of sugar, instead of borrowing cups from neighbors. The elementary-school teacher who is going through a divorce has been spending a great deal of time at her local Home Depot recently. "I'm becoming a tool-belt girl," she proudly declared. It is the perfect image—each of us owns all the tools he or she needs, and we carry them with us. There are times when a tool belt is exactly what someone needs. It is especially comforting in the middle of a divorce. But like a gun belt in the Old West, there is a time to hang it up and reach out for the help of friends.

CHAPTER 4

Left Out

An Organism under Stress

We described the experience of feeling left out as a powerful engine of human emotion and behavior that works in opposition to the American ideal of self-reliance and standing apart. Now we want to take a little time to understand the source of that experience's power in the dynamics of social isolation.

An understanding of the experience of feeling left out comes from a convergence of three lines of thought—evolutionary psychology, the neurobiology of attachment, and common sense. Human beings, both as a species and as individuals, survive only through attachment to one another. In fact, as biological organisms, we are designed to become attached to one another. States of broken attachment are thus both physiologically stressful and psychologically distressing. We all know the emotional distress that comes with broken attachments. But in times of loss, we are also more vulnerable to illness and more at risk of dying. And each of us responds to distress in one of two ways—either make an effort to reconnect (by repairing the shattered attachments or forming new ones) or give up and become depressed (in psychoanalytic jargon, that type of depression is called an anaclitic depression).

The experience of being left out is the first step on the way to the biologically determined terror of detachment. It triggers a set of alarms warning of impending disaster, and it also sets in motion a whole array of compensatory behaviors, including efforts to get back in (if not to the groups that left us out, at least to some other groups) and efforts to minimize the stress and distress by redefining the ones who leave us out as unessential attachments (the who-needs-them? strategy). If those strategies fail, a variety of psychiatric symptoms emerge that reflect a primitive fear (*primitive* in the neurobiological and evolutionary sense), the fear that if we are alienated from the group, we cannot survive.

We will flesh out the details of this argument and then look at a series of elegant experiments by a group of social psychologists who are beginning to understand the particular changes in thinking and behavior that follow an experience of social exclusion.

Before we take on the science of the argument, however, let us connect it to one woman's encounter with broken attachments: Megan and her husband had worked hard all their lives. They did not catch many breaks, so when Megan developed a chronic illness in her early sixties, around the same time that her husband was laid off from his job, they decided to take what meager savings they had and spend as much of the year as possible in a cabin in the Northeast Kingdom in Vermont. "Our little piece of paradise," she called it, so beautiful and so peaceful. Years before, Megan had been successfully treated for depression with a combination of psychotherapy and medication. She usually dropped by from time to time to check in, renew her prescription, and talk over how her life was going. Her last visit broke the pattern. Life in the peaceable Kingdom had spiraled down into a dark depression. She had been very depressed for months, perhaps more depressed than she had ever been before.

"I knew I should call you but I was just too discouraged. And I couldn't face the drive down. I think my depression is just getting worse as I get older. The medicine doesn't work anymore. I'm so afraid you're going to tell me that my only option is ECT [electroconvulsive therapy]. April was the worst. I didn't get out of bed for almost the entire month."

What emerged was a picture of a life that Megan had imagined would be suffused with peace and quiet but instead felt to her like living on the dark side of the moon. As we talked about her spending more time around Boston, reconnecting with her friends, even taking an art class, her mood visibly brightened. Almost as an afterthought, we wondered whether something had changed at the beginning of April. Her eyes widened with recognition. Since the end of March, there had been no communication between Megan and her brother, her only living sibling. The event that transformed a mild depression into a severe one turned out to be a rift with her brother over politics.

He was her older brother, the one she had always looked up to while they were growing up, "the smart one," the only person in the family to go to college. He was also a military man and a pilot, the kind of man who made a kid sister feel protected and safe. Their rift came when Megan, now a savvy woman in her sixties, finally rejected his "guidance." "Enough already!" she had said, in effect. "You know I don't agree with your politics. Stop sending me all those damned articles." "About time!" some people might say. In her early sixties, Megan was old enough to make up her own mind. That was certainly what she thought. And yet, when she'd told her brother to back off and he had, she didn't just feel lonely. She felt scared. The world she lived in had suddenly become more dangerous. The change was visceral, not intellectual. Megan herself knew it made no sense. For all their adult lives, she and her brother had been separated by most of a continent and vast differences in their political and religious beliefs. That hadn't mattered. She had still felt embraced and protected by him. But when the weekly propaganda stopped coming, she felt as though she had dropped out of his thoughts and had been cast out of a magical circle of protection.

Yes, part of the job of any decent psychotherapist is to help someone like Megan grasp the irrationality of her thoughts. If a therapist jumps there too quickly, however, he or she might not notice that Megan's irrationality flows directly out of human nature, out of the instincts and brain structures that have allowed human beings to survive in a dangerous world. Megan will be better off once she gains some control over her gut reactions and stops responding as though her safety really does depend on the protection of her brother. Megan will also be better off once she recognizes her reaction as simply human rather than pathetic and sick. In fact, Megan was immediately happier when she realized that she did not want to be left out of her brother's life and might be able to do something to get back in—without needing to hide her own political opinions.

Mental health treatment and research has paid a great deal of attention to issues of attachment and to the consequences of broken attachments. However, the experience of being left out has been relatively neglected, even though being left out sounds an unpleasant alarm about the potential breakdown of attachments. It is a transitional state; it may turn out to be just a bump in the road in a thriving relationship, or it could be an important first step to really being left out in the cold.

The feeling of being left out seems so fundamentally trivial, so whiny and babyish. Teaching children how to handle this inevitable emotion is the business of preschool teachers, isn't it? And for most of us, learning how to manage those moments on our own takes place in the gruesome cauldron of early teenage cliques. As adults, we are supposed to be beyond all that. Suggesting to someone that feeling left out still plays a shaping role in his life can sound like an accusation of childishness if it's done without tact. But to come to grips with the effects of feeling left out, we each have to recognize that both the feeling itself and the reactions to it are deeply human. The experience is a part of human biology that no one ever fully outgrows; at best, one just gains a certain degree of mastery over it.

There may be another reason why the experience of being left out gets short shrift in psychotherapy theories and practice. Feeling left out is an issue for many psychotherapists. It is often part of the developmental path that leads someone to an interest in becoming a psychotherapist. Those wonderful moments when a person feels happily and effortlessly embraced by a group are not the moments that cultivate curiosity about what makes other people tick. It's the moments of feeling like they're on the outside looking in that gets many people thinking about the fascinating and terrifying messiness of human relationships. What better way to master lingering worries about being left out than to become an expert in relationships? And then, from the safety of expertise, to be slightly dismissive about the emotional impact of those feelings?

(We suspect that something similar might be true for the sociologists whose vital research we reference throughout the book. Sociology, like psychotherapy, is a discipline that combines privileged access to details of the lives of others with a professional position that involves standing on the outside looking in. But we have not made a study of the personal lives of sociologists.)

Common Sense

"It's a dangerous world out there. You won't get far alone." There's some common sense for you. That's what makes the loner hero in the last chapter so heroic. Without the help and protection of others, the odds of getting a toehold in either the natural world or the social world are pretty much zero. There are just too many threats, too many disasters, and too many predators. You need someone to cover your back (or your ass, or whatever part you have to risk exposing to get ahead). You need the strength of numbers, whether it's a clan or a gang or a union or a country. Being part of a group carries its own dangers, but you sure want to be able to have a group around you when you need it. That's a lesson we all learn early in life, and should we forget it, we'll get plenty of opportunities to relearn it.

Learning that we need to belong to groups for our safety and survival would be useless if we didn't also learn what it takes to be part of a group. One of the basic requirements is the ability to monitor how we are doing as parts of the groups, whether we fit, whether we are trusted, whether we can trust the others in the groups. In other words, if a person wants to be able to count on the protection of a group, that person needs to be pretty good at monitoring his safety within the group. In particular, he needs to be alert to any signs that his status as a member of the group is threatened. That alertness is simple common sense. What it means is that most of us learn to be very sensitive to small cues that we are being left out, because being left out *matters*. It matters in a way that is basic to our functioning as human beings. This may not be true for every group that we encounter, but it certainly is for some of them. The need for a special sensitivity to the threat of being left out is simply part of the human condition.

Evolutionary Psychology

Evolutionary psychology builds bridges between a commonsense understanding of behavior and a biological understanding. It begins with some version of the concept developed by John Bowlby, the British psychiatrist who began the scientific study of attachment and bonding in human infants and children. He called it *the environment of evolutionary adaptedness*—the environment that, through natural selection, shaped our biology, including the biology of our brains. Evolutionary psychology attempts to find the biological basis of modern behaviors, particularly those behaviors that are ill-suited to the current world in which we live, by examining our species' adaptation to the demands of a much earlier world. Over the last twenty years, evolutionary psychology has produced a mix of profound insights and whimsical speculations—the latter including such gems as the assertion that it is so hard to get most young children to eat their spinach and broccoli because in the environment of evolutionary adaptedness, most dark green plants were poisonous.

An evolutionary perspective on the experience of being left out starts with two simple facts. First, human beings are remarkably helpless at birth and remain in a state of extreme dependency for a very long time. Second, even as adults, single human beings are unlikely to survive for very long alone in a dangerous world. If human beings were not endowed with both the capacity and the impulse to connect with others, we would not have a chance. And that endowment must be embedded in our biology. The first fact underpins the biology of infant attachment (especially mother-infant attachment). The second fact is the bedrock of an emerging biology of social connectedness. Together, they begin to explain the persistent power of feeling left out, even when the strength of that emotion seems to make no sense in the immediate situation. The frightening power of that feeling is part of our biological nature, an evolutionary adaptation that made it possible for our species to survive.

The importance of the mother-infant bond to basic survival is clear enough to most people that it needs no further comment, but new and exciting parts of the story are now emerging. The biological structures and processes underlying the mother-infant bond, structures and processes that evolutionary reasoning predicts must exist, are just beginning to be understood. (We will look at them in the next section.) And an understanding of the evolutionary importance of bonds that extend to a wider social group is also just emerging. Because this part of the story is less self-evident (particularly in a culture of rugged individualism), we will linger a little longer over the idea before turning to the emerging hints about its biology.

Stanford sociologist Patricia Barchas put it simply and powerfully twenty years ago: "Over the course of evolution the small group became the basic survival strategy developed by the human species for dealing with almost any circumstance."[1] Roving bands were the basic human unit, not unlike the survival strategies of other primates. If the small group is the basic survival strategy, however, then groups themselves become part of the environment of evolutionary adaptedness. In other words, over time, humans adapted to their own reliance on groups, and those adaptations in turn became part of humanity's biological heritage. As Harvard linguist Steven Pinker explains, "Groups were certainly part of our evolutionary environment, and our ancestors evolved traits, such as a concern with one's reputation, that led them to prosper in groups."[2] Even more basic to prospering in a group than a concern with one's reputation (though closely related to it) is a concern with being left out. It is the ultimate threat for any creature who has evolved to use small groups as a basic survival strategy. We need to be very well endowed with the ability to monitor our fellow creatures for the emergence of that threat, and we need to be greatly distressed when we discover it, or even simply imagine that we have discovered it. As we shall see, new research on social exclusion confirms an exquisite sensitivity to the threat of being left out, even in trivial situations. The strength of our responses to trivial instances of being left out, a level of response that does not seem to fit the immediate situation, suggests that it reflects our nature and our evolutionary adaptation, not just our stupidity.

The most intriguing work on evolutionary biology and social connection comes from British scientist Robin Dunbar. His most startling suggestion is that language, our species' most defining and sublime achievement, evolved for the purpose of allowing us to gossip.[3] By *gossip*, he means the social rather than utilitarian use of language—"Did you hear what they did?" rather than "There's a herd of bison down by the lake." According to Dunbar, gossip plays the same role for humans that grooming behavior does for other primates. It creates bonds between individuals that go beyond the basic reproductive units of sexual partners and their offspring. It creates groups. And language can bind together larger groups than grooming can. It all sounds widely speculative, but Dunbar has some interesting and surprising data. He has looked at the relationship of neocortex size and group size in primates (the neocortex, literally "new cortex," is the part of the brain most recently added by evolution and most involved in thinking and other higher functions). As group size increases, so does the size of the neocortex. Dunbar also found that neocortex size does not correlate with other higher-level activities, such as hunting and building shelters, just with group size. The same correlation between neocortex size and group size exists in nonprimate carnivores, and even in bats (vampire bats turn out to be the most social, altruistic, and big-brained). Dunbar reasons that we have developed large neocortices as well as language itself to deal with the social complexity that comes from using larger groups than other primates use as our basic survival strategy. The group provides us with safety, but it also creates its own dangers, as individuals and subgroups maneuver within them. In short, humans have survived in a dangerous world because of a wonderful set of adaptations, but these adaptations include being perpetually vigilant for the dangers that can arise *within* a group, including the possibility of being outmaneuvered and left out.

The Neurobiology of Attachment

If evolution has shaped us into social beings, then we should be able to discover a biology of social connection, along with a biology of our response to social disconnections. The explosive growth of neuroscience over the last decade is starting to give us some tantalizing clues.

Currently, we know more about the biology of our strongest attachments—mother-infant bonding and romantic love—than we know about the wider net of social connections, but those powerful bonds are a good place to start. A clever set of studies has been done by Andreas Bartels and Semir Zeki, two neuroscientists at University College London. In one study, they used neuroimaging techniques (fMRI) to investigate "the neural basis of romantic love."[4] They recruited subjects who professed to be "truly, deeply and madly in love." They showed each subject a picture of the beloved and three pictures of friends who were the same sex as the beloved, and then the researchers compared patterns of brain activity. The body of the report is a detailed listing of a dozen or so brain structures that were differentially activated or deactivated by lovers versus friends. The importance of the study, however, has more to do with what it *was* than what it found. As the authors themselves write, "Here we have for the first time tried to explore the neural correlates of personal relationships." In other words, science is just beginning to allow us to see what our brains are doing when we are in social relationships. There are no neuroimaging studies yet to show us what our brains are doing when we get left out of social relationships, but those will come.

Bartels and Zeki's findings become more interesting in a second study.[5] They performed the same experiment as earlier, except this time they used mothers of young children, showing pictures of the mother's own child, another child of the same age (whom the mother had known for just as long), and some adult friends. The patterns of activation and deactivation in maternal love turn out to be similar to, but not identical with, romantic love. Not exactly surprising yet, but there is more. In both states of love, activity increased in the areas of the brain associated with reward and pleasure (the striatum, the middle insula, and the dorsal part of the anterior cingulate cortex—more on this in a moment), and activity was suppressed in the areas of the brain responsible for negative emotions *and* for social judgment (the mesial prefrontal cortex, the parietotemporal junction, the temporal poles, and the amygdala). With both maternal and romantic love, the machinery of the brain that's responsible for making critical assessments of other people gets shut down. To put it another way, love really is blind. But pity the beloved should circumstances suddenly unleash the areas of the brain responsible for social judgment.

Now all this may seem very far from the experience of being left out, but it is not. Although as yet there are no neuroimaging studies to go along with it, the same suppression of critical judgment has been shown to take place within groups. Group members make more favorable assumptions about people in their own group than they do about people outside the group. These favorable expectations distort both information processing and memory: we tend to forget the bad things that fellow group members do and remember the good things.[6] People also "understand" the causes of success and failure in group performance in whatever way places their own group in the best possible light.[7] Just as much of the same machinery is used for both maternal and romantic love (evolution tends to be efficient in that way), it is likely that the same brain mechanisms that lead to suppression of critical thinking about children and lovers is also used to suppress critical thinking about members of an in-group. Since it takes active suppression of the brain's capacity for critical thinking to maintain a favorable opinion of the people we love and consider "with us," there is always the risk that something will cause the machinery of critical thinking to click back into gear. Once again, the price of being part of a group is the perpetual danger of being left out.

What about the pleasures of attachment, the activation of the reward system of the brain? Here, the imaging studies of Bartels and Zeki link up with a large body of research in animals. The reward system is a set of structures and pathways in the brain me-diated by the neurotransmitter dopamine (the mesocorticolimbic-dopaminergic reward circuit). It is the brain system that leads people to keep doing something they like because it gives them pleasure. Addictive drugs like cocaine lead to dopamine release in the reward system. The dopamine-mediated experience of reward and pleasure is a big part of what makes those drugs addictive. The same reward system has been shown to be crucial to social attachment in animals—both mother-infant attachment and pair bonding (the animal version of romantic love). Either ironically or unsurprisingly, depending on your perspective, substance abuse and social attachment use the same brain machinery to generate pleasure.

Thomas Insel, a neuroscientist at Emory University, reviewed this connection in a paper provocatively titled "Is Social Attach-ment an Addictive Disorder?"[8] His answer was a tentative yes—not that social attachment is a disease, but that substance abuse hijacks brain pathways that have evolved to encourage social at-tachment. Insel's starting point was a suggestion by the evolution-ary biologist Paul MacLean that at the level of basic neurobiology, substance abuse serves as a substitute for social attachment.[9] Two important points about being left out follow from these ideas. First, the pain that a person experiences when a social bond is bro-ken, whether it is the death of a loved one or a social rejection, is not some Johnny-come-lately experience created by overly ro-mantic love stories or a too-sensitive culture. It is a pain that is felt in the deep structures of the brain, and it reverberates through bi-ology and experience in complex and powerful ways. Second, the connection between social isolation and substance abuse, which we'll discuss in more depth in a later chapter, is built into the brain and is not just a casual consequence of loneliness.

Another piece of the emerging picture of the neurobiology of attachment is the two neuropeptides oxytocin and vasopressin, which function as neurotransmitters. These two chemicals are found only in mammals. They help manage stress, particularly the stress of birth and the postpartum period, and are crucially involved in social bonding. Both oxytocin and vasopressin reduce social anxiety and fear, leading animals to approach rather than avoid each other. Oxytocin in particular is released during positive social interactions and has a calming effect on both behavior and physiology. As we will see in chapter 8, social connections are good for our health: they make us less likely to develop a wide variety of diseases and more likely to live longer. Oxytocin is a good candidate for the chemical bridge between emotional experiences and the physiological processes that lead to these health benefits.[10] There is also good evidence that when bonds are broken through death or divorce, immune functions deteriorate and the risk of illness increases.[11] Again, oxytocin may play a mediating role in the physiological effects of shattered bonds.

A clear mediator between the stress of broken bonds and the body's immune response is the hypothalamic-pituitary-adrenal axis (HPA), the central brain and hormone system responsible for managing stress. It is fairly straightforward to evaluate stress by measuring components of the HPA response, and the HPA response to social separation has been studied in a wide range of primates and other mammals. A simple summary is that the disruption of social relationships is physiologically stressful to mammals, but the nature of each physiological response depends on how much the animal cares. Researchers distinguish between attachment and affiliation, essentially a distinction between intense emotional bonds (attachment) and less passionate connections (affiliation). The disruption of an attachment bond leads to rapid elevations of HPA activity. The disruption of affiliative bonds affects HPA activity over a much longer time frame.[12] Both are stressful, but in different ways, so when we talk about the experience of being left out, we need to distinguish between being left out by people one cares deeply about and being left out by people who matter in less intensely emotional ways. How exclusive the category of really mattering is depends on the species. Young sheep but not young goats react to separation from their peers with a rapid increase in HPA activity.[13] Sheep tend to hang out together more than goats, so their peer group matters more to them. We suspect that in this regard, some people are more like sheep and some more like goats. Yet as we shall see, even being left out by people who don't matter at all is surprisingly disruptive.

The neurobiology of attachment is still a very young science, but it is growing fast. Perhaps the most important conclusion to draw at this point is that there *is* a neurobiology of attachment. And therefore there is also a neurobiology of disrupted attachments, a neurobiology of loss and social rejection and feeling left out. These experiences are important socially, psychologically, *and* biologically. They are not just the domain of oversensitive crybabies.

Social Exclusion in the Laboratory

The left-out experience is never very far away in ordinary life, but it is hard to capture in the laboratory. Social psychologists Roy Baumeister and Jean Twenge have collaborated in a series of clever experiments to do just that. The term they use is *social exclusion*, and they use two different experimental situations to mimic it.[14]

In the first situation, college students are brought together in small groups and given fifteen minutes to get to know one another, using a set of questions to guide them. They are then separated, told that the experimenters are forming groups of members who like and respect one another, and are asked to name the two people (from those they just met) with whom they would most like to work. The participants are then randomly assigned to be "accepted" or "rejected" by the group. The accepted participants are told, "I have good news for you—everyone chose you as someone they'd like to work with." The rejected participants are told, "I hate to tell you this, but no one chose you as someone they wanted to work with."

In the second situation, college students take a personality test and are given accurate feedback on their extroversion scores. That feedback is then used as a segue to assign each participant randomly to one of three groups. In the first group, the future-alone condition, the participant is told,

> You're the type who will end up alone later in life. You may have friends and relationships now, but by your midtwenties, most of these will have drifted away. You may even marry or have several marriages, but these are likely to be short-lived and not continue into your thirties. Relationships don't last, and when you're past the age where people are constantly forming new relationships, the odds are you'll end up being alone more and more.

By contrast, students in the future-belonging condition are told they are likely to have lives filled with rewarding relationships, stable marriages and friendships, and people who care. There is also a third group, the misfortune condition. Those students are told they are likely to be accident-prone later in life, with lots of misfortune. No prediction is made about their relationships so the experimenters can see if people respond to plain bad news differently than they do to bad news about future aloneness.

We have described the experimental setups in detail because we want to give a sense of the flavor of the students' experiences. Imagine hearing someone who is in a position to know the truth speak the words that place you in the rejected group or the future-alone condition. They are deeply unsettling words, more unsettling than they should be, if you are reasonable about all this. After all, one message is just a prediction about the distant future, and everyone knows how unreliable that usually is. And the other message is simply that you have been left out by a few strangers to whom you talked for fifteen minutes and who don't really matter to you at all. The psychologist Albert Ellis, who developed a precursor of cognitive therapy in the 1950s, wrote a book with the hopeful title *A Guide to Rational Living*. He claimed that a huge amount of unhappiness was caused by a small number of irrational ideas. One irrational idea was that people believe that everyone should like them. If the participants in Baumeister and Twenge's experiments were rational, they would have just shrugged and gone on with life as usual. But they, like all of us, were not rational about being left out. Being left out touches something deep in our biological nature. The "excluded" students did not just shrug and get on with things. These two artificial and, in some ways, trivial experiences of social exclusion had remarkable consequences.

In a series of papers published over four years, Twenge and Baumeister found the following:

1. Social exclusion makes people more aggressive. In the laboratory, excluded students were more likely to torpedo job applications of people who they believed had insulted them and more likely to blast opponents in video games with what they thought were painful, punishing noises. Their increased aggression was not only toward people they thought had insulted them, but also toward neutral people, the equivalent of innocent bystanders.[15]

2. Social exclusion causes self-defeating behavior. Excluded students were more likely to choose risky long shots that were rationally the wrong choice. They were more likely to procrastinate by reading magazines or playing video games when given the opportunity (and good advice) to prepare for a test. They were more likely to make unhealthy choices —eating more cookies, choosing a candy bar over a gra-

nola bar, reading *Entertainment Weekly* instead of accepting feedback on how to improve their health, opting to laze around instead of exercise.[16]

3. Social exclusion reduces intelligent thought. Excluded students showed declines in performance on complex cognitive tasks that required efforts at logic and reasoning. Their scores on IQ tests also dropped.[17]

4. Social exclusion leads to a state of mind that "avoids meaningful thought, emotion, and self-awareness, and is characterized by lethargy and altered time flow" (time weighs heavy and seems to slow down).[18]

5. Social exclusion leads people to quit sooner on frustrating tasks.[19]

Baumeister and Twenge believe that the central consequence of social exclusion (leading to all of these effects) is an impairment of self-regulation—the ability to monitor one's behavior and adjust it to circumstances. They also suggest that one of the main functions of self-regulation is to enable a person to get along with others. An important question is this: Does rejection lead people to be *unable* to self-regulate, or *unwilling* to? The answer seems to be *unwilling*. When excluded people in these studies are paid for difficult tasks, their performances improve again. It seems that social rejection leads people to give up and stop trying.

We should tie up a few loose ends. A reasonable assumption is that social exclusion has such powerful effects on behavior because being left out makes people feel depressed or bad about themselves. But Baumeister and Twenge found, over and over again, that the effects of social exclusion were not caused by either increased depression or decreased self-esteem. The change in behavior after social exclusion took place in the absence of any signs of emotional distress. This point is important. Feeling left out dramatically changes how people function without their noticing that they feel particularly bad about it. Another important point is that these behavioral effects are specific to social exclusion. Those in the misfortune condition, the students who were told that they'd have lots of accidents in later life but not that they'd be alone, did not respond in the same way. Finally, since it is hard not to worry about the "excluded" students in these experiments, the researchers offer reassurance that all the participants were debriefed before leaving the lab and did not have to live with the feeling of rejection for more than a few hours.

In-Groups and Out-Groups in the Laboratory

Another crucial piece of the left-out experience is the formation of in-groups and out-groups, the cause of so much left-out misery. If the evolutionary argument is correct in stating that a small group was the basic survival strategy of the human species, the formation of small groups should be a part of our nature. Even the most casual observation of the social life of our species supports that argument, whether we turn our attention to schools, the workplace, neighborhoods, or (with more direct consequences to survival) urban gangs and ethnic or religious violence. There also have been a small number of experiments that look at the formation of in-groups and out-groups.

The most elaborate one has a wonderful name—the Robbers Cave Experiment, which is also the title of the book that describes the study. In the early 1950s, the social psychologist Muzafer Sherif constructed a remarkable field experiment to study intergroup conflict and conflict resolution. He set up a three-week summer camp for twenty-two fifth-grade boys in an isolated area of the San Bois Mountains in southeastern Oklahoma, on the site of a two-hundred-acre Boy Scouts camp that was completely surrounded by the Robbers Cave State Park. (The report on the experiment is filled with nostalgic black-and-white photos of boys pitching tents and playing tug-of-war.) Over the first few days of camp, two groups were arbitrarily created, assigned to separate tasks, and kept physically separate from each other. A few days was all it took for a powerful sense of us-against-them to emerge, with intense rivalry and hostility between the two groups. There was name-calling, negative stereotyping, boys refusing to have anything to do with people in the out-group, even boys holding their noses when an out-group member was nearby (after all, these were eleven-year-old boys). Hostility took hold and it would not let go. The experimenters arranged for increased contact between the two groups. There was no decrease in hostility. Only when the boys were faced with a series of crises and challenges that they could overcome only by the two groups working together (for example, an experimenter-contrived water shortage) did intergroup hostility decrease and cooperation begin.

It is breathtakingly easy to create in-groups and out-groups. And not just with American boys at camps. In a state school in Bristol, England, fourteen- and fifteen-year-old boys and girls were asked to estimate the number of dots projected for a split second onto a screen. They were then told that some people consistently overestimated the number of dots and some consistently underestimated them. They were also told which group they were in themselves. Next, they were given another task and told to assign monetary rewards and punishments to everyone; they could choose among several strategies to decide how the money should be distributed. One strategy maximized the total payoff for both groups, one maximized the in-group's payoff, and one maximized the difference in payoffs between the two groups (favoring the in-group). Most subjects chose the third strategy—having *their* group win on points—even though they clearly understood that they were sacrificing both the general good *and* the maximum winnings of their group.[20] Now, this is a remarkable result: you are assigned to a group based on a characteristic that simply and clearly does not matter, and, immediately, being a member of that group does matter. Favoring *your* group over the *other* group also suddenly matters.

The Bristol experiments are powerful evidence that human beings use us-against-them as a fundamental way of understanding the world and organizing behavior. And if the world is organized that way, an alertness to our finding ourselves on the wrong side of us-against-them, finding ourselves left out, must also be one of our essential social tools. When do we begin to see the world this way and organize our behavior into us-against-them strategies? A doctoral student at Harvard found evidence of in-group versus out-group behavior among preschoolers in day-care centers.[21]

Surrounded Yet Left Out

Although we've taken an excursion into group politics, we don't want to lose sight of the possibility of people feeling left out right at home, in the bosom of their families. These converging lines of reasoning—common sense, evolutionary psychology, neurobiology, and social psychology—lead us right back to the idea that feeling left out is a major engine of human emotion and behavior, fundamental to our way of being in the world. It is so fundamental that the smallest of hints or miscues or misunderstandings can catapult someone into feeling left out and trigger all the maladaptive behaviors that goes along with the feeling. It can happen to you when you are surrounded by the ones you love, even the ones who love you back.

Remember Freud's beloved Oedipal child. His painful discovery is not that he is unloved, just that his parents also love each other. Seeing the love between others can make someone feel left out, even if he knows that the others love him as well. And those Oedipal children have their revenge eventually. We once joked about writing a paper called "The Oedipal Crisis of the Aging Parent." It would be about the moment (actually, the many moments) when beloved parents discover that they are at the periphery, not the center, of what is most vital and exciting in their children's lives. Most parents expect and hopefully welcome the moment when their children fall in love, but that on-the-outside feeling can sneak up in so many other little ways. A while ago, Richard was playing music with a grown-up child and his friends. At a certain moment, he realized that he was on the periphery, both musically and interpersonally. He wasn't really left out. They were all playing together, and the children were quite kind. It's just that he was left out of the center of things. Or felt he was.

That trivial musical moment is instructive. No one has to *be* left out to *feel* left out; a person simply has to believe that the bonds between others are more alive or intense or intimate than their connection with him. That is all it takes. In families, in groups of friends, in the workplace, in politics, the discovery that some people are more *in* than others (whether that's accurate or an illusion) changes everything. It touches something primitive in human nature. The individual feels offended. He feels endangered. The instinct is to step back and, often, to retaliate. A vicious cycle of hurt and exclusion can easily take hold. Out of these small moments, like a hurricane gaining force over warm waters, come family feuds, shattered friendships, ruthless maneuvering, and even wars.

In the next two chapters, we will look at how some of the natural brakes on this destructive process have been taken away by two dramatic changes in American life: the rise in geographical separateness and the increasing reliance on electronic technologies for social connection. Both of them reduce the day-to-day, face-to-face contact that's most likely to stop in its tracks an exaggerated sense of being left out; a casual chat, a shared task, a relaxed smile, or a friendly look can put ill-chosen words in a benign light. Eternal vigilance against being left out is the price humans pay for using the small group as a basic survival strategy. We creatures of small groups are also endowed with the capacity to connect and to nurture our connections. We just need to be careful that our alertness to the threat of being left out does not become a hair trigger for paranoid snits. As we shall see, human neurobiology makes that overreaction easier to avoid when there is a full range of sensory data from the other person—exactly what is missing with geographical distance and electronic communication.

Those tempting steps away from the frenzy of everyday life and toward the ideal of self-reliance unfortunately also eliminate the processes that keep us from feeling too left out. We step back, and then, inevitably, notice that the connections among others are stronger than their connections with us. We forget that it was our choice. Or, more accurately, we chose to step back, but we certainly did not expect that the others would go on happily without us. So we each feel left out, a state of mind with surprising power and consequences.

CHAPTER 5

Free at Last

American Living Arrangements

Americans' quest for independence has taken a curious turn. Every year, more of us live alone. The one-person household is on the rise. The U.S. census first asked about the size of the household in 1940, and in every census since then, the percentage of households consisting of one person living alone has risen steadily. In 1940, it was 7.7 percent. In 2000, it was 25.8 percent. The places where people are most likely to live alone have also shifted. In 1940 and 1950, it was the far West—Alaska, Montana, Nevada, and Washington—the open spaces of the fading frontier.[1] Now one-person households are most likely to be found in major metropolitan centers. Manhattan leads the pack: 48 percent of all households on the island are one-person households.[2] Our own hometown of Cambridge, Massachusetts, is not far behind, at 41.4 percent.[3] In 1970, Philip Slater wrote, "Even within the family Americans are unique in their feeling that each member should have a separate room, and even a separate telephone, television, and car, when economically possible."[4] Slater spotted the trend, he just didn't carry it far enough. Separate rooms are no longer sufficient. We would rather have separate homes.

Slater was right about our desires but was wrong about their uniqueness. The United States is not the only country experiencing a rise in one-person households. Western Europe is witnessing the same phenomenon. Housing statistics from the European Union in 2003 found that one-third of all Europeans live alone, and current projections suggest that by 2007 it will be just under 40 percent.[5]

The tilt toward one-person households is reshaping our social world and will also reverberate through our planet's ecology, affecting our use of resources and the size of our environmental footprint.

Living Alone in a Social World

Living alone does not have to mean being lonely and depressed. An acronym was coined in the 1990s—*LATs*—to describe couples who are "living apart together." Living alone can lead some people to widen their social worlds. But living alone can also be a trap. As Slater warns, "We seek more and more privacy, and feel more and more alienated and lonely when we get it."[6] What determines which way living alone breaks for a person?

College dorms offer an opportunity for a study that, to our knowledge, has never been done. Some are set up with single-person rooms off a long corridor. Some have multi-person rooms or suites. It would be interesting to know if either architectural arrangement creates a wider social network. Our suspicion is that the averages would be about the same, but that the averages would hide very different outcomes for different types of students. Single-person rooms (*singles*, in dormitory jargon) tend to throw students out of their rooms in search of people to talk to. These rooms probably lead to wider and more diverse contacts for outgoing students but very dense solitude for those who choose not to emerge. Multi-person rooms and suites are more self-sufficient. They can create more insular social worlds, but they also let shy students ride the coattails of more sociable roommates, reducing the need for social initiative and nerve from every single student.

In other words, a corridor of singles is likely to look more socially vibrant but hide a greater number of socially disconnected students than a corridor of multi-person rooms. We suspect that the same is true in life outside of dormitories, but singles are then even more difficult for the temperamentally shy—at least in college, almost everybody is looking for friends.

We know some wonderfully engaged people in single-person households. They are also among the most socially skillful people that we know. *Skillful* is the right word. These friends are not all naturally outgoing, but they have all acquired the skills of actively engaging with others. They take initiative in both creating and maintaining connections. Lois Ames, a psychotherapist and poet in her seventies, tells us that she discovered a simple and unfortunate rule of thumb after her divorce forty years ago, and she has been teaching it to women ever since: a single woman must make three times as many phone calls as she gets and offer three times as many invitations as she receives if she wants to maintain her network of friends. One might hope that the ratio has dropped over the last forty years as divorce has become so common, but Ames does not believe it has.

Now *single* meaning "unmarried" is not the same as living alone. Currently only about half of individuals who are single live alone. Ames's point about initiative and effort applies to both groups, however. Either *you* make it happen or it doesn't happen. The challenges of living alone may actually encourage people to take initiative and develop more active approaches to maintaining connections. That hope was supported by the one published survey of the effect of solo living on social connection in the United States. It is an old study, based on statistics from 1978. Living alone had no *consistent* negative effect on social integration, and there was some support for a compensation effect, that is, people living alone worked harder to stay connected and had "heightened levels of friendly contact outside the dwelling unit."[7] A 2005

British report comes to the same overall conclusion: nearly half of those surveyed said they see parents, siblings, and friends about the same amount as they did before they lived alone, and 27 percent said they now spend more time with friends.[8]

On the other hand, surveys that ask people how they remember spending their time may not be the best way to find out how they actually spent their time. A better approach is to have people record their daily activities using Internet-connected time diaries. A recent (and large) time-diary analysis from a group at Stanford University found that "individuals living alone are less likely to spend time with family, friends, and on socializing."[9] We will have more to say about this study in the next chapter, but it raises questions about a certain degree of wishful thinking in at least some self-reports of social engagement. Even those more reassuring self-reports, however, show many people in trouble, as well as a new source of pressure on the world's resources.

A Few Details

We have more details about solo living in Great Britain than in the United States, perhaps because a greater emphasis on social welfare planning there has led to more studies of the shift in living arrangements. The *Unilever Family Report 2005* summarizes one trend with the phrase "lonely men, empowered women."[10] Men living alone are more likely to *feel* lonely[11] and to experience negative effects on their health.[12] Working-age men are currently the fastest-growing group of people living alone, probably because relationship breakdown often leads to men living alone and women living with children. And while most nonretired individuals who live alone believe it will be a temporary state for them, women who live alone are more likely than men to continue to live alone. And for all groups, once a person lives alone, he or she is more likely to continue doing so than to move into any other type of living arrangement.[13]

It is a little risky to apply British studies to American life. In Britain, nearly a third of people living alone see their parents two to three times a week.[14] The simple geography of family relationships is clearly different in the two countries. Less physical separation in a smaller country may actually mitigate some of the effects of living alone.

Some of the British findings, however, make intuitive sense when applied to life in the United States. They take us back to our college-dorm analogy. Historically, men have had wider social networks then women, but their social networks emerge from their activities in the world. Women are more likely to see social connections as a part of life that requires initiative and active attention. Men tend to make friends early in life in circumstances that throw people together, such as school or the military, and to see their circle of friends get smaller over time as individuals drop away. Women tend to make new friends throughout their adult lives.[15] In other words, on any given day, a man living alone in an apartment is more likely to stay alone in an apartment, and a woman is more likely to call someone. The gender differences are interesting and even have important public health implications, but we all know that when it comes to how actively people pursue social connections, knowing someone's gender does not tell you much. Some people are likely to drift out of contact when circumstances don't automatically provide that contact. Living arrangements are the result of an increasing freedom of choice, and some of us are casualties of the choices we make.

We must not exaggerate the blissfulness of free choice. Not all solo living is the result of affluent singles following their dreams. In Britain, individuals who live alone are more likely to be either poorer or richer than the average person.[16] British researchers even suggest that an increase in single-person households is a significant factor in rising income inequality. While we don't have formal data for the United States, our strong impression is that the

situation here is very similar. Two streams are feeding the rising
tide of single-person households. One group consists of individuals whose range of choices is rapidly expanding. It is a group whose
members have the luxury of considering other choices. The second group consists of people whose other options have fallen
away. Their ability to make choices is more dependent on shifts in
the economy or social policy. Clearly, it would be a mistake to treat
both groups the same way. Nevertheless, there are certain consequences that are similar for both groups: the impact on personal
relationships, the effect on individual psychology, and the strain
on the world's resources.

Stepping Back, Getting Stuck

Most people who live alone hope that the arrangement will be
temporary, but living alone sets in motion certain processes that
make it hard to find a way back to living with others. An old phrase
explains why: we get *set in our ways*. The *Unilever Report* contains
the following quotes from participants in some of its focus groups
(the first is from a woman and the second from a man):

> "I do wonder what it will be like if I ever live with a
> boyfriend, I'm so used to my own space, and I think that
> having to compromise would be very hard."

> "It [solo living] makes you selfish in a way."

Other participants also "expressed a fear that having enjoyed the
benefits of living alone would make them less able to live with others in the future." These were the traditional fears about "con-
firmed bachelors" and "elderly spinsters," stereotypes of those
who had lived alone too long. They are fast becoming the ordinary
fears of ordinary young adults.

Looking back, we realize that we caught an early glimpse of a changing world years ago, when we had dinner with distant relatives who had just brought their daughter to Boston for her freshman year of college. They arrived with a large U-Haul truck of belongings only to find that the daughter's roommate (and her family) had already filled the room so completely that there was no hope of moving their daughter's things in. An angry visit to the housing office led to the daughter's transfer to a single by the end of the day. At the time, we thought we were witnessing one of those dramas of family eccentricities that make family life interesting and embarrassing. We now understand that we were peering into a future in which more and more children grow up "used to my own space" and used to filling that space with their own possessions. And yes, compromise is very hard.

As psychiatrists in a town filled with colleges, we are often asked to write letters saying that a student *needs* a single for psychiatric reasons. There *are* students who are much better off rooming alone for psychiatric reasons, but there are not that many of them. Twenty years ago, we would get that request from an occasional patient who was really in trouble. Now we get demands for those letters from patients (and their families) simply because some students find it a little inconvenient to figure out how to get along with roommates. The clear message is that developing the skill of living with others (other than doting parents) is no longer important.

Faced with rising numbers of students seeking psychiatric exemptions from living with others, we find ourselves teaching our patients about the importance of learning to live with others, helping them to understand that this requires skills that can in fact be learned, and then helping them learn those skills. At the center of these discussions is the idea of "staying limber"—a phrase that seems to work well for most of our patients. What we are trying convey is the need for a certain kind of flexibility, a willingness to adjust (at least a little) to the inevitable quirkiness of another human being at close quarters. We also talk about how staying limber is essential not just for dormitory living but for future work and family life. (What greater demand is there on someone's capacity to adjust to the inevitable quirkiness of another human being than parenting a child?)

A new study places this drama in a disconcerting context. Narcissism (roughly equivalent to self-centeredness) is on the rise among today's college students. Using a standardized questionnaire called the Narcissistic Personality Inventory, researchers found that scores have been rising steadily since 1982. Two-thirds of students now have above-average scores for narcissism, a 30 percent increase since 1982.[17] There is no other example in empirical psychology research of personality changing as rapidly and dramatically. Something big is happening here, and it makes the give-and-take required to live with others much harder to find. How simple it is instead to live alone and spend time with others only when it is congenial and convenient. We are free to come and go. We are with people only when we want to be. How could that be a bad thing? Won't our relationships become more alive and exciting when we share time with others only when we are "into it"?

Well, yes and no. We wrote a book about marriage with the subtitle *The Natural Ebb and Flow of Lasting Relationships*. Any relationship that lasts and deepens over time must have some way of hanging on through the inevitable rocky patches. Without practice in finding the way through trouble with another person, without a lived experience that it is both possible and worthwhile to hang on, a person is likely to turn away and start spending time with someone else who, for the moment, is wonderfully congenial and convenient. Modern modes of communication facilitate that shift. A new study called "Media Multitasking Among American Youth"[18] confirms that it is what most people do most of the time. A college student recently told us that everybody checks e-mail and talks on the phone at the same time. How simple, then, when a conversation hits an awkward bump, to shift attention to one of the other simultaneous tasks and, in a tiny way, begin to write someone off. Sociologists sometimes distinguish between *friendships of commitment* and *friendships of convenience*.[19] Most people always have both kinds, but many are tilting further toward friendships of convenience. That tilt helps explain why surveys that ask people how many friends they have report encouragingly high numbers, while the General Social Survey finds that more and more Americans have no people that they confide in. We are only likely to talk about matters of importance with people whose connections to us have stood the test of time.

How We Think When We Are Alone

> For a long time I liked it that way. I enjoyed coming and going without telling or explaining, being free. I enjoyed listening without talking. I enjoyed being wherever I was without being noticed. But then when the dark change came over my mind, I was in a fix. My solitariness turned into loneliness.
>
> Wendell Berry, *Jayber Crow*[20]

Unfortunately, solitariness makes that dark change more likely. Mihaly Csikszentmihalyi, a pioneer in what has now come to be called positive psychology, conducted a series of groundbreaking studies with a very simple design. When a beeper went off, a subject noted what he or she was doing and how he or she was feeling. Across thousands of subjects in a wide range of cultures, Csikszentmihalyi found that most people who were left on their own with unstructured time tended to become bored, fretful, and self-critical.[21] Even though most of us say we are happiest on weekends and vacations when we have nothing we have to do, it turns out that we are wrong. Csikszentmihalyi was interested in a state that he called "flow"—those moments when our awareness of

time disappears and we are completely and passionately lost in activities we care about. Those activities may be solitary or social,
but they are crucial to a sense of vitality in our lives. Those people
who have solitary flow activities available to them are partly protected from the fretfulness of being alone because time spent by
themselves is filled with meaning and purpose. But the meaning
and purpose of even the most engrossing of activities decays too
easily in solitude. Enthusiasm is a hard emotion to sustain if it cannot be shared with others. Even a master of solitary flow activities
needs to know that at least one other person cares. When we spend
too much time alone, the sense of meaning and joy even in the activities we love can start to slip away. Sitting in an apartment alone
trying to learn an elusive new song on the guitar is a very different
experience from the same struggle when someone calls out from
the next room, "Hey, that sounds good!" And for those of us who
lack solitary flow activities, the decay of meaning and joy in an
empty apartment is almost immediate.

Another way that being alone changes our thinking is a major
theme of this book: we start to feel left out and, at the extreme,
even a little paranoid. Almost everyone who has ever lived alone
in an apartment (the authors included) can remember a night (or
sometimes many nights) when the sound of loud music coming
through the walls of a neighboring apartment wrought a "dark
change" in the mind with devastating suddenness. The skillful or
lucky ones will quickly find friends who can help keep the left-out
feeling at bay. The others are in for a grim night that starts with
the straightforward recognition of being left out of one particular
party but can quickly spiral down into feeling like a loser. And
when things get really bad, their self-pity can morph into rage at
the neighbors who don't give a damn about them or, even worse,
are intentionally tormenting them and laughing about it. A wonderful teacher of ours, Leston Havens, once said that the closest
most of us can get to understanding a paranoid state of mind is to

remember the experience of getting out of bed in the middle of the night and stubbing a toe on the dresser. He may be right, but the experience of sitting alone in an apartment late at night and listening to a party next door is a close second. A more heart-breaking example, one we have seen too many times, is the elderly person living alone and actually slipping into paranoia, convinced that every noise is the intentional act of a malevolent and hated neighbor or landlord. Simply having a roommate to complain to can make all the difference in the world, restoring perspective and maybe even a sense of humor.

A natural extension of the left-out feeling is an increasing re-luctance to seek out social connection. Calling people takes just the kind of social confidence that aloneness tends to undermine. That is the wisdom of Lois Ames's three-times-as-many rule: it re-minds you to keep on calling because that's just the way the world works, not because you're a loser. If you are living with others and your social connections fray, it is easy to let yourself be carried along on someone else's connections until your own get repaired. ("Come on. Don't just sit around. Come out with us tonight.") And when you let yourself be carried along, you are much less likely to have the collapse of confidence that leads a person to bur-row into aloneness, if that is your "natural" tendency.

We have a patient who looks like the most socially confident woman in the world. Cathy can walk into a coffee shop, bar, or corner newsstand, and pretty soon people light up in conversa-tion with her. When she speaks professionally, she regularly holds large audiences spellbound; she may be nervous before she starts, but once she gets under way, she tosses her notes aside. Her skill at quickly engaging others saved her from a chaotic and deprived childhood. When she started treatment, there was a lot to be very worried about, but loneliness was not anywhere on the list. She lived alone, yet her life and her days were filled with people. But when she lost her job, she experienced a failure of nerve, a failure of finances, and soon a complete collapse of her seemingly vital social world. Living alone had once seemed so effortless for her, but suddenly it was a very big problem. There was nothing built into Cathy's days that brought her into contact with others. She stopped taking initiative. For a while, she could count on the initiative of friends, but that began to fade as friends became discouraged. When someone lives with others, like it or not, he or she has to reckon with them and somehow respond to their concerns. Phone calls and e-mails are much too easy to ignore. Eventually Cathy's friends stopped calling, and she came to feel so embarrassed about ignoring them for so long that she couldn't imagine calling even when she wanted to.

Her psychotherapy helped. It may have been lifesaving, since she was becoming seriously depressed and thinking about suicide. Her weekly appointment was the only human contact that Cathy could count on without her having to do something to make it happen. She made good use of that contact—to understand what had gone wrong, what was her fault and what was outside of her control, what she had to do to rebuild her life, and how to hold on to a sense of hope and possibility. Finding a way back into regular contact with friends and family was a crucial part of the plan. It worked, despite some frightening moments, partly because psychiatrists have some specialized skills and talents in helping people with depression. But a lot of what took place in Cathy's psychotherapy sessions looked like the kind of support and perspective that friends and family give one another all the time. In fact, it looked a lot like the kind of support and perspective that Cathy's friends had often given her in the past. There is no doubt in our minds that Cathy's life had been saved by friends long before she ever consulted a psychiatrist. Solo living placed all those potentially lifesaving friends far away, somewhere beyond the front door, and it also placed Cathy somewhere outside her friends' line of sight. Living with others is no all-purpose shield against depression. It can, however, provide resources that are simply and crucially *there* at the moment they are needed most by someone who is slipping toward depression and withdrawal.

In his novel *Rabbit Is Rich*, John Updike writes, "What you lose as you age is witnesses, the ones that watched from early and cared, like your own little grandstand."[22] The watching and caring together can make such a difference in our lives. The watching and caring together lead to something even more precious than our own little grandstands. When people both watch and care, they will step in to offer help when help is needed. Updike is right—some of the grief of old age is the sense that there is no longer anyone watching or caring. Living alone, until recently the realm of the elderly, can create a prematurely precarious state where no one is watching. And with no one watching, the caring can arrive too late.

Eco-Consequences

Our choice of living arrangements also has an impact on the earth. As the social resources that each of us once had easily at hand are reduced, the material resources that each of us wants to have easily at hand are simultaneously increased. When our relatives arrived with a large U-Haul truck of possessions for their college-bound daughter, we caught an early glimpse of not only a changing social scene but also an emerging ecological threat. Living alone, whether in a single in a college dorm or in a one-person household, each of us wants to own many possessions that are automatically shared when people live together. The ongoing shift toward youth in the demographics of one-person households is an important reason for the threat. In the words of British researcher Jo Williams, "Previously, the typical one-person householder was the widow, often on a tight budget and thrifty. The rise in younger, wealthier one-person households is having an increasingly serious impact on the environment."[23]

In a 2006 study,[24] Williams provides a detailed analysis of the effect of household size on per capita consumption of energy, products, packaging materials, land, and waste production. Her data covers England and Wales, but the broad outlines of her conclusions certainly apply to all Western capitalist societies: resource consumption goes up dramatically as household size decreases. Although the precise amount that resource consumption increases varies by category, moving from a four-person to a one-person household more or less doubles the consumption of resources per capita. Two-person households were somewhere in between. The people in the households were all adults, so the effect has nothing to do with small children needing less. Spreading out adults into one-person households is a powerful way to use up the earth's resources more quickly. It will also make a contribution to global warming—one-person households used 77 percent more electricity and 54 percent more gas per capita than four-person households. Once people understand that the increasing numbers and decreasing ages of single-person households is an *international* trend, they will understand that "solo living's eco threat"[25] (to quote a headline in the *Guardian Unlimited*) is to be taken seriously.

Marketing consultants have already spotted the trend and write about it not with anxiety but with breathless excitement. "One Is Fun—and Lucrative Too," proclaims a headline in Food&DrinkEurope.com.[26] The "breaking news on food marketing and retailing," as the electronic magazine's tagline runs, goes on to report that "single-person households [are] spending 50 percent more per person on CPG (consumer packaged goods) than two-adult households." An American report[27] announces that "those who live alone are an attractive market in certain product and service sectors," with alcohol consumption receiving special attention ($314 per year for the single-person household as compared with $181 in households of two people or more). The

Yankelovich Monitor "found that across all age groups, members of single-person households are far more willing to spend money on themselves than others their own age who are in other living arrangements."[28]

There may be an opportunity for successful business models (and government programs) that reduce the ecological threat of single-person households. The full title of Jo Williams's 2006 paper is "Innovative Solutions for Averting a Potential Resource Crisis—the Case of One-Person Households in England and Wales." After presenting convincing evidence for an emerging crisis, Williams proposes a range of policy suggestions to prevent it. Her ideas fall into two broad categories: policies that encourage the design and construction of more ecologically sound one-person households, and policies that encourage alternatives to one-person households, such as communal and collaborative housing. Many of her proposals are specific to Great Britain, but the dual goals—lessening the environmental impact of people living alone and creating desirable alternatives to solo living—are ones we would be foolish to ignore.

CHAPTER 6

The Technology of Relationships

A Brief Review

A friend of ours, Hal, has a blog. With words and pictures, he opens up parts of his life, sometimes with startling intimacy. It is not exactly a public space, although anyone can stumble upon it. Our friend assumes he is speaking to friends and family. And with friends and family, there is space to respond to him, and people do. Not long ago, his mother died. He wrote about loss and bewilderment and nightmares. He invited and received caring responses from his friends. No one reading his blog would say that he is using a technology that lets people drift farther apart.

We wrote about this same friend ten years ago. We used him as an example of how friendships can grow and thrive through shared projects, even in overbusy lives. In Hal's case, it was through a revolving series of weekend construction projects that he shared with a small group of friends. The practical benefit of improving one another's houses was real enough, but it also provided cover for spending time with friends. Hal has a knack for friendship, whether he uses a blog or a nail gun to keep it going. Notice how he uses his blog. He is not using it to create a disembodied community in cyberspace. He is using it as just one more tool to connect with the same old people he has been seeing all along—the same old people that he continues to take the trouble to see in person. We think Hal is on to something about social networking on the Internet that formal research is just starting to confirm. The Internet works best when it's used to extend other ways of connecting rather than replace them. We also think that even Hal is taking some risks with his friendships in his enchantment with a new tool. People's enchantment with the latest technologies, operating in the middle of already busy lives, can easily lure them away from those old-fashioned ways of connecting that require two bodies in the same place, with all the sensory and communicative richness and subtlety that brains expect in human dealings with one another. As our colleague Sherry Turkle, a psychologist at the MIT Media Lab, said to us, "You're saying, *Yes, but we have bodies.*" That *is* what we are saying, and we will try to explain why.

The Rich Get Richer and the Rich Get Poorer

In our drift apart, is technology part of the solution or part of the problem? The question touches our fascination with technological change as an engine of both good and evil in our lives. It fuels our hopes for building a better future and stirs up the dread we sometimes feel watching the disruption of the familiar patterns of lives. Friends whose eyes glaze over when we talk about social connections come back to life when they are arguing about the effects of the Internet or cell phones. There is objective research on the social effects of the Internet. The problem is that we can sort the published studies into two piles: one pile that shows the Internet creating greater social connection, and one that shows the Internet creating social isolation.

The argument will eventually shift from sociologists who are trying to peer into the future to historians who are trying to understand the past, but, regardless, the argument will continue. Did the arrival of television gather together family members from separate rooms so they could have a shared experience (as some articles in popular magazines cheerfully proclaimed)? Or did it destroy the family's capacity for more active engagement with one another through conversation, shared music-making, and the like (as dour intellectuals grimly predicted)? Did the automobile and the telephone make it possible for people to stay connected despite increasing geographical separations, or did the inventions play key roles in creating those separations? You can squint at the facts from different angles and argue for a net gain or a net loss but you'll probably end up settling for both. The same is true of the Internet. Nonetheless, there are some reasonable conclusions we can reach when we put the dueling surveys side by side.

The most encouraging surveys on the social effects of Internet use come from the Pew Internet and American Life Project. We mentioned the Pew project in chapter 1; in contrast to the General Social Survey, it found evidence for generally large social networks, and we discussed some possible reasons for the conflicting results. We now turn to its specific conclusions about the effects of Internet use:

> Rather than conflicting with people's community ties, we find that the Internet fits seamlessly with in-person and phone encounters. With the help of the Internet, people are able to maintain active contact with sizable social networks, even though many of the people in those networks do not live nearby. More, there is media multiplexity: The more that people see each other in person and talk on the phone, the more they use the Internet.[1]

Let us spell out the two parts to this conclusion. First, the Internet allows people to have larger social networks. Second, connecting to others through the Internet does not reduce spending time with people in more old-fashioned ways. The Pew story is that those rich in friends just get richer with the Internet.

On the top of the other pile are studies from Norman Nie and his colleagues at Stanford. They also study the effect of Internet use on people's social lives. Their conclusion could not stand in greater contrast to the Pew study:

> The more time people spend using the Internet, the more they lose contact with their social environment...As Internet use grows, Americans report they spend less time with friends and family, shopping in stores or watching television, and more time working for their employers at home—without cutting back their hours in the office. A key finding of the study is that the more hours people use the Internet, the less time they spend with real human beings.[2]

Nie's story is that the rich get poorer, squandering their connections with friends and family.

The argument is about what has been called the displacement model, or the replacement hypothesis (each group uses its preferred phrase). Does time on the Internet replace other forms of social connection, or does it supplement it? Both studies are based on standard survey data: asking people questions about what they generally do. In a separate paper, Nie adds intriguing data of another sort: time-diary studies. The study uses Web TV to have subjects record what they were doing during specific blocks of time on the previous day, rather than recording their impressions of what they have been doing over time. One of the things we have come to appreciate as psychiatrists is how seamlessly most people fool themselves (and others) about how they actually spend their time. The time-diary approach reduces the opportunity for wishful thinking to reshape people's stories about what they do. There is still the opportunity simply to lie, but there is less room for self-deception. Based on time diaries, Nie concludes that "for every hour spent on the Internet at home [in contrast to Internet time at work] . . . individuals are spending an average of almost 30 fewer minutes with their family." The effect is even larger (forty-one fewer minutes) for each hour of use on the weekend. Internet use creates similar reductions in time spent with friends and in social activities, although the amount of time lost is less than with family members.[3]

What should we conclude from this ongoing argument? First, researchers who investigate complicated questions tend to find what they expect to find. That troubling statement is supported by a great deal of evidence, most of it from medical research where more than just academic reputations are at stake. We are not saying that most researchers are charlatans who fudge the facts. Most researchers are honorable people confronting complicated questions. Nonetheless, faced with the complexity of the world and the inevitable messiness of complex data, researchers find it practically impossible not to give a little more weight to results that fit with what they already believe. There is even a name for that tilt: confirmation bias.

Second, some people (like Hal) are great at connecting with others. They do it in person, they do it on the phone, they do it on the Internet, and they do it well. We don't have to worry about them. Except maybe we worry about their lives' increasingly frenetic pace as they willingly add more and more to their lives and make it all work by multitasking, moving faster, and sleeping less. A 2006 study called "Media Multitasking Among American Youth" finds (no surprises here) that American youth multitasks a lot and that computer activities are the "most multitasked."[4] The Pew report suggests that the Internet does not replace other forms of socializing, just TV watching and sleep. Those rich in friends may get richer on the Internet, but finally they may just get tired.

Third, some people (unlike Hal, but like the people in Nie's time-diary study) are trading in-person contact with family and friends for Internet time. Should we worry about them? Certainly we should worry if they are trading away social time for the many nonsocial uses of the Internet. By now, most of us can think of at least a few sad individuals who have made that trade. But what about the ones who are spending social time on the Internet: chatting, e-mailing, visiting MySpace or Facebook? Are they richer or poorer for the trade—in social capital, in intimacy, in happiness? What does it mean to connect with others on the Internet rather than in person? What difference does physical presence make anyway in human relationships?

Our Bodies, Our Faces, and Our Brains

Today's news happens to report that the social-networking site Facebook is the sixth-most-visited site on the Internet, "with 24 million monthly unique users."[5] How can we be worried about the future of social networks when a single social-networking site has twenty-four million people a month creating and sustaining connections?

Over the years, many patients have asked us some version of this obvious question: "How important is it for me to be here for these sessions? Can't we just talk by telephone?" Sometimes it is a question of necessity—a temporary placement in another state, a crisis while on the road. Sometimes it is a sign of the forced or cherished busyness that we have been writing about—"I could do this by phone from my desk but there's no way I could take the time to actually get to your office." It is a fair question. Psychotherapy is a deeply personal relationship, but it seems to be about words ("talk therapy"), and words seem to travel well in electronic form. Why not just use the phone?

There are articles written about telephone therapy and analysis, usually by clinicians reporting their own successes. Kasia Kozlowska, a child psychiatrist at the Children's Hospital in Westmead, Australia, recently spoke to us about her use of videocon-ferencing to consult to families across her country's vast distances. Elise Snyder, an American psychoanalyst, reports that there is an emerging interest in psychoanalytic training in China and is or-ganizing American analysts to offer telephone analyses (via the In-ternet service Skype) to trainees in China. People are bridging the world to connect to others in deeply personal ways. Why indeed should anyone bother to actually be there?

Our own experiences with telephone therapy (and occasional interludes of e-mail-based treatment—we confess that we are too set in our ways to develop the rhythms of instant messaging) is something of a mixed bag. Yes, we have had extremely successful treatments by phone, but the longer the sessions go on, the more pallid they become. This observation will seem like common sense to most people, but what about the famous image of a psychoana-lyst staring off into space while listening to the voice of a patient who is lying on a couch? Psychoanalysis is a treatment *designed* to eliminate most channels of sensory information, supposedly in the service of better understanding. How does that make any sense? And why is a telephone any different? Skipping over a longer ar-gument that would be of interest only to psychoanalysts, we will just make two quick points. First, it really does feel different to be listening to someone who is next to you, even when you are not looking at each other. We all know that. The difference in feeling reflects the richness of our sensory experiences in the presence of another, which creates an urgency that gets filtered out by most technologies. That is why so many people these days get restless and start checking their e-mail while talking on the phone. Sec-ond, psychoanalysts often have to work very hard to pay attention. The benefits (for some patients)—the freedom to follow the flow of their own thoughts, unencumbered by all the intricacies of face-to-face encounters—makes the work worthwhile, but psychoanalysts are paid for that work and trained to do it. That is what keeps them (hopefully) from checking *their* e-mail while the patients are talking.

Just as it takes extra effort for a psychoanalyst to be truly attentive and responsive to the voice of a patient, it takes a great deal of extra effort for anyone to be truly attentive and responsive electronically. It is hard to maintain that extra effort over time. It comes as no surprise that electronic communication and multitasking go hand in hand. There is simply not enough sensory input to engage us over time, so we naturally start to fiddle with other things. Who has not learned to recognize the subtle breaks in the smooth flow of a phone conversation that signal that the other person is multitasking—simultaneously checking e-mail or searching the Internet or (an old-fashioned image) sorting through papers on the desk? Telephone therapy seems to work best when the stakes are very high for both parties. If someone's life is at risk or if there is the chance to have something precious that would otherwise be impossibly out of reach (like psychoanalysis in China), then it is much easier to leave your e-mail alone. As Elise Snyder wrote in an e-mail, "Whatever the debate about the efficacy of telephone analysis—there in NO other solution at this time for China." Electronic being-there is better than not being there at all, but that does not make electronic being-there the equivalent of physical presence. And yet who among us has not decided that a visit to a friend or relative was no longer important because we already talked on the phone or exchanged e-mails?

A patient of ours has a best friend who has been fighting cancer and beating the odds for many years. The two women talk by telephone every day, but for the past year our patient has not visited her friend. Visits, which used to be frequent, have been discouraged by the dying woman. The reasons were never explicit, but they seem to be a mix of shame about the state of her body and shame about the state of her home. Recently our patient talked about a terrible sense that she had become cold and uncaring because she didn't feel for her friend as strongly as before. She wondered about some core defect in her capacity for love and friendship. The more she talked, however, the clearer it became to her that it was hard to feel as loving toward her friend when she no longer saw her, took walks with her, or simply sat by her bed. There are just the earliest glimmerings of research to suggest that the difficulty our patient has in feeling deeply connected to someone she is not physically near reflects something that is not at just her core, but at the core of all of us—our brains and our human nature.

In an essay in the *New York Times*, the science writer Daniel Goleman points to "a design flaw inherent in the interface between the brain's social circuitry and the online world." He continues:

> In face-to-face interaction, the brain reads a continual cascade of emotional signs and social cues, instantaneously using them to guide our next move so that the encounter goes well. Much of this social guidance occurs in circuitry centered on the orbitofrontal cortex, a center for empathy. This cortex uses that social scan to help make sure that what we do next will keep the interaction on track... But the cortex needs social information—a change in tone of voice, say—to know how to select and channel our impulses. And in e-mail there are no channels for voice, facial expression or other cues from the person who will receive what we say.[6]

Goleman is trying to understand the phenomenon of flaming on e-mail—sending a message that one would usually have the good sense not to send by any other medium. He cites research con-

ducted by Jennifer Beer at the University of California, Davis, on
the social function of the orbitofrontal cortex. Beer's work supports the hypothesis that this part of the brain is necessary for the
self-monitoring that lets us avoid or repair social mistakes.[7]

What information do we need to stay on track socially? "The
orbitofrontal cortex receives inputs from all the sensory modali-
ties: gustatory, olfactory, somatosensory, auditory, and visual. Visceral information is also received by the orbitofrontal cortex..."[8]
In less technical language, the orbitofrontal cortex uses *all* of the
senses, all the physical information available, to monitor and modulate social behavior. Our brains appear to be wired to make getting along with other people an inherently *physical* enterprise. No
wonder it is so easy to get it wrong by e-mail. We also begin to understand why the telephone, which at least gives us tone of voice,
works better than e-mail but not nearly as well as sitting together
on the front porch.

Goleman hopes the answer lies in better technology. "One
proposed solution to flaming is replacing typed messages with
video. The assumption is that getting a message along with its
emotional nuances might help us dampen the impulse to flame."[9]
No doubt it would be better—if the goal is to reduce flaming.
But if the goal is to reach the full potential of human responsive-
ness, the orbitofrontal cortex will still be trying to manage with a
terribly impoverished experience of connection. Like a Skype psychoanalysis stretching between China and the United States or a
videoconference consultation to a family with a troubled child in
the Australian Outback, it is wonderful to be able to reach people
whom we had no way of reaching before. The worry is that we will
forget the importance of reaching at least some people through
the fullness of a shared physical presence.

Music and the Technology of Connection

One of the curiosities of the human brain is how it responds to music. Music can induce some of the deepest experiences of sharing and connection, from the everyday ("You *have* to listen to this new song I just heard") to the transcendent ("as if the eternal harmony were communing with itself, as might have happened in God's bosom shortly before the creation of the world"[10]). The musician-turned-neuroscientist Daniel Levitin notes that "music is unusual among all human activities for both its *ubiquity* and its *antiquity*. No known human culture now or anytime in the recorded past lacked music."[11] Music is also always shared through the technology of the day, whether it's the innovations of instrument makers in ancient times or the iTunes and iPods of today. Music seems perfectly designed to travel electronically, to create shared experiences that transcend geography. And it does, better than ever before. A patient of ours who is a young musician came in recently excited about iLike, which (we learned) is an Internet service that offers "social music discovery," a sharing of musical explorations that efficiently bypasses the need for someone to bother to say, "You *have* to listen to this new song I just heard." The service, iLike, simply scans the music libraries of friends (and like-minded strangers), tells you what they are listening to, and "helps you connect musically with your friends and the broader iLike community."

What can music teach us about social connection? First, new forms of connection that transcend geography really are evolving. Second, it can take us a while to realize what gets lost in these new forms of connection. Daniel Levitin's group looked at the different responses to a music video among those who only heard the audio, those who only watched the video, and those who did both. The level of tension that a listener experienced during a particular musical passage was dramatically changed by the addition of visual information about the performer's emotional state while he was playing the passage.[12] The experimental result is not exactly a big surprise, but it does remind us that technology can transform our experiences without our paying very much attention to the change. As we happily use earbuds or speakers to fill our lives with more music than ever before, we don't bother to remember that what we are hearing is not exactly the same music that we'd hear if we could see the performance. The connection made with the music and the musician is not the same connection. Better than not hearing the music at all, but still not the same.

So Daniel Goleman was right about flaming. The solution is technical. Just wait until video replaces e-mail. But Daniel Levitin is not really interested in the power of music videos. As the *New York Times* reported, his own musical life led him to wonder, "Does the brain experience a live performance differently from a recorded one?"[13] We (along with Levitin) know that the answer has to be *yes*. Levitin is just trying to tease out the details scientifically. No music lover would ever take seriously the claim that a music video is the equivalent of a live performance. Something is still missing, something that engages all of the senses in the experience and locates it fully inside the body. It is that phenomenon, two embodied brains connecting with each other, that geographical closeness provides—living in the same house, chatting with a neighbor on the street, going to a concert with a friend. The Internet gives us something of great value. But not that.

Pornography and the Technology of Connection

The technology of connection also blurs any easy distinction between public and private space. Remember our friend Hal's blog. As we said, it is not exactly a public space, but it is not a private space either. Hal is a wonderful photographer, a skillful writer, and an occasional Web site designer. He is speaking to friends and family on his blog, but he has also created a showcase for his artistry. If strangers wander in and admire or feel moved by what they find there, Hal would not consider them unwelcome intruders. The blog is probably a little like the private correspondence of famous writers—written to the recipients, but sent with an eye to the hoped-for volume of collected letters. When publication is forced to wait until the distant future, however, private communications have time to play themselves out first. On the Internet, public and private moments collide in time.

Jeff is a psychiatrist in his early thirties. He recently stepped into the world of Facebook even though, as he said, "It's not my generation's thing." He described the experience as "really intense but also superficial." His juxtaposition of the words *intense* and *superficial* caught our attention. He was trying to describe an important paradox of digital communication, so we asked him to tell us more. The intensity came because he was suddenly "back in touch with people you thought you were all done with." In particular, he was looking at pictures and commentary from his old best friend who had become a football star and stolen away Jeff's high-school girlfriend. And here was his old friend, still looking like a star in pictures that seemed to locate him at the center of an exceptionally vibrant social whirl. "It's like you get to do it over again!" is how Jeff described it. The chance for a do-over from adolescence is not exactly great news for most of us, but it is definitely intriguing and very hard to resist. Jeff felt his body tense up and his heart rate rise when he sat down at his computer and reentered that old competitive arena one more time.

But if the experience was emotionally intense, why did Jeff say it was also superficial? Did he mean that he was replaying an old teenage game that should have been over by then? No, that wasn't it. In fact, he was now playing the adult version of the game. His sense of his status and success in his present life was very much on the line. That part of the story leads right back to its intensity. It was superficial, Jeff said, "because it's writing on a Web site!" He

was pointing to the Internet's invitation to play out intensely personal dramas on a public stage with an audience looking on, some
of them known participants and some of them unknowable lurk-
ers. That is one of the important ways that the Internet invites
us to re-experience an aspect of teenage friendships and romance
that most of us were relieved to leave behind when we escaped
from high school. A startling intimacy can certainly emerge on a
public stage, but it is always crafted with an awareness of the audience. We don't have vocabulary to distinguish public intimacy
from private intimacy, but we know that they are different and that
the difference has something to do with a shift from developing
reciprocal connections to just getting attention.

A patient who works in marketing for a high-tech firm was
talking about a series of business meetings. It turned out that the
customers ran companies that operated major pornography Web
sites. Perhaps a little defensively (the patient's own habits leaned
more toward reading history than viewing pornography), he took
a few minutes to give a brief historical review of how pornography,
the major income-generating presence on the Internet, has regularly been the driving force behind technological innovation. It is
not surprising that technology that was developed to increase the
flow of traffic to porn sites is a technology that leaves us feeling
all muddleheaded about what is public and what is private. The
pornographer's skill is to create the illusion of intimacy and privacy where neither exists. The pornographer's skill is to create the
feeling of being there, an intensity of experience associated with
the physical presence of another person, while leaving the viewer
still alone. The pornographer's skill is very real, along with the
technology to support it, and it works well. Data from Internet
ratings services make that clear. In 2000, "about one in four regular Internet users, or 21 million Americans, [visited] one of the
more that 60,000 sex sites on the Web at least once a month—

more people than go to sports or government sites."[14] Today, the number of visits and the number of sites are even higher. Each of those visits usually has a curious double effect on the (mostly male) visitors—it eases their loneliness even as it leaves each of them feeling more alone. That double effect—the paradoxical experience of connection and aloneness, of an intensely private encounter and a public performance—is the same thing that Jeff noticed when he described Facebook as intense but superficial. It would be comforting to conclude that the disconcerting mix of connection and aloneness, the bewildering collapse of the boundary between public and private, arises only when technology is used poorly. However, pornography is not a misuse of the technology. It is the technology's major financial backer. We may find that the difficulties surrounding human connection on the Internet are built into the technology itself.

Social Strategies

Technology changes our physical experiences of other people. It changes how we think about our relationships. It also changes our social strategies. Here are two intriguing bits of information: customers of online dating services go out with less than 1 percent of people whose profiles they study, while participants of speed-dating events go out with more than one in ten of the people they meet. Maybe speed daters are just more desirable than online daters. Speed-dating certainly takes more nerve, which might pull in better-looking players, but science writer John Tierney offers another hypothesis based on his wonderful concept of the Flaw-O-Matic, "a mechanism in the brain that instantly finds fault with a potential mate." Online dating kicks the Flaw-O-Matic into high gear: "They can spend all day finding minute faults in hundreds of potential partners." The speed-dating situation creates a different effect: "The people at these events realize that there aren't an infinite number of possibilities. If they want to get anything out of the evening, they have to settle for less than perfection. They also can't help noticing that they have competition, and that their ideal partner just might prefer someone else."[15]

We think Tierney is right on the mark. As "loneliness experts," we are very clear about the fact that online dating has been a boon to some of our loneliest patients. A colleague of ours nearly overflowed with her enthusiasm for it. "I have three patients in my practice who are married and one more with a live-in lover from online dating. And they'd tried everything else first—Lunch Dates, that woman who charges so much for fixing people up, everything!" Online dating offers an increasingly important service in our socially fragmented world. But as Tierney points out, it also changes how we think about people. The power of the Internet as a social universe is in its seemingly limitless possibilities. The trap of the Internet as a social universe is also in its seemingly limitless possibilities. With limitless possibilities, why settle for any one of them? Something better might be just around the corner. We have a few friends who, likable as they are, share an irritating trait. Whenever we plan to get together, they never commit themselves until the last minute, even when the plan was their idea. We finally admitted to ourselves what was going on up to that last minute. They were cruising for a better deal. Something better might still turn up and they didn't want to be tied down. The Internet shifts cruising for a better deal into overdrive.

The problem with roommates and neighbors and coworkers (and spouses and parents and siblings) is that people are stuck with them, at least for a while. Yet being stuck with a person is ordinarily how relationships deepen. Because someone is there, you talk together, do things together, get to feel just a little more connected to each other, even weather an argument or two. You don't scratch your head and wonder before each encounter, *Is this the best option?*

The strongest bonds are usually between people who were thrown together in one way or another—family members, old friends from school, teammates, service buddies—rather than people who were carefully chosen.

The working assumption of modern life and especially modern commerce is that more choice is better and that people with more choices are happier. New research suggests strongly that the assumption is simply wrong. As psychologist Barry Schwartz writes in an article titled "The Tyranny of Choice," "Logic suggests that having options allows people to select precisely what makes them happiest. But...abundant choice often makes for misery."[16] Schwartz draws a graph of "net feelings," which translates as roughly equivalent to happiness, as number of choices increase. Starting with "virtually infinite unhappiness" when there is no choice, he shows an encouraging surge of happiness with a few choices, and then after that happiness heads south with more and more choices. He offers several factors to explain that graph, beginning with "opportunity costs," which is essentially a person's awareness of what might have been chosen instead, which triggers second-guessing, regret, and wishful thinking. Most research on the psychology of choice has focused on consumer choice in the marketplace, but it is easy to extend the results to social choices. With more and more opportunity to search for exactly what we want, our lives can become dominated not by joy but by regret. Perpetually cruising for a better deal is (of course) not the road to happiness. We all know that. But it is exactly the social strategy that the Internet encourages, and we willingly go along with it. Imagine the wonders that await with just one more click!

Social networking on the Internet seductively trades depth for breadth. Barry Schwartz's graph explains why it is so seductive. A little more breadth makes us happier. What we don't notice is when we have reached the tipping point. We end up adopting a social strategy designed for a world of limitless possibilities without recognizing that it can create a very lonely world, a world of perpetual seeking and unending regret.

A Step Ahead of the Technology

Sherry Turkle, at the MIT Media Lab, studies the effects of emerging technologies on our psychological selves. She writes: "We are witnessing a new form of sociality in which the isolation of our physical bodies does not indicate a lack of connectedness... The connectedness that 'matters' is determined by our distance from available communications technology."[17] We are glad that she put the word *matters* in quotes. The question is whether people can have the benefits of this new form of sociality without letting the old forms slip through their fingers as though they no longer matter. We, the authors, are just as attached to the Internet as the next person and just as unwilling to disconnect. We just worry that many people's ideas about what digital technology offers in the way of human connection is a step ahead (at least) of what that technology actually delivers. Over the last three decades, researchers in wide-ranging fields of study have begun to document how much connectedness matters: to physical health, to mental health, to happiness, and even to the body politic. We know practically nothing about which of the many forms of connectedness matter or how those different forms of connectedness matter in different ways. Someday technology may indeed make physical proximity in living arrangements irrelevant. But it would be a terrible mistake to start to live as though that day has actually arrived.

Bodies, Bricks, and Mortar
(and Refrigerators and Energy and Packaging...)

We ended the preceding chapter about American living arrangements by looking at the ecological consequences of sixty years of the relentless rise in the number of one-person households—the increased use of energy and land and major appliances and packaging materials, the ecological side effects of physically isolated living arrangements. These side effects would have to be reckoned with even if we were to conclude that digital connections might someday encompass most of what "matters" in human relationships. Not only do we still have to deal with our bodies in a digitally connected world, we also still have to deal with our bodies' impact on the physical world. Sherry Turkle talks about the "tethered self" that digital connections have created. We can't forget that we are still tethered to the earth as well.

In the early days of the World Wide Web, a standard conviction was that the most successful online merchants would be the ones who also had bricks-and-mortar stores. That may no longer be true for selling on the Internet, but it is not a bad strategy for social networking. Using the Internet, we will sometimes make near-miraculous connections to people who would not otherwise have existed for us. But we would be fools to tear down our old-fashioned bricks-and-mortar friendships, connections shaped by the proximity of two bodies in a physical world.

CHAPTER 7

Love and Marriage in a Busy World

The General Social Survey of 2004 is not uniformly bleak. It offers an encouraging bulletin about the state of marriage in this country. The GSS found that marriage is the only relationship in which people are *more* likely to discuss important matters with each other than they were two decades ago.[1] We confide less in parents, siblings, children, other family members, coworkers, comembers of groups, neighbors, friends, advisers, and "others," but at least we are confiding more in our spouses![2] That sounds like good news about marriage, and it is. As a dismal point of comparison, consider the picture of a typical marriage in the 1920s taken from the Middletown studies, a remarkably detailed portrait of life in an anonymous midwestern town provided by five decades of sociological research. Most married couples in the 1920s spent little time in conversation, bickered when they were faced with a shared decision, and, when the bickering was done, "often lapsed into apathetic silence."[3]

By contrast, most married couples these days feel that their spouses are their closest confidants[4] and their best friends. When that stops being true, couples are more likely to get divorced than to lapse into apathetic silence. Some of the health of marriage today is the result of a vigorous pruning of unhealthy marriages (unfortunately, a large number of potentially healthy marriages also get eliminated along the way). But some of this apparent health comes from the sacrifice of all those other possible confiding relationships on the GSS list. In other words, the increase in communication within marriages comes in part from the process of stepping back—from the crowd and the fray—and stepping into lonesome-hero dreams, the family version—more Daniel Boone and *Little House on the Prairie* than Clint Eastwood. Cocooning is the couples' version of social isolation. It does increase closeness in marriages. It also increases the fragility of marriage, the burdens placed upon marriage, and, over time, it increases the likelihood of both divorce and loneliness. The critical question is this: When do social ties compete with one another and when do they strengthen one another? Both processes are clearly at work in the complex relationship between the vitality of marriage and the vitality of other social bonds.

Cocooning: Stepping Away Together

The word *cocooning* entered the language in the 1990s, courtesy of the marketing consultant Faith Popcorn. We stumbled upon a version of the phenomenon at around the same time while doing a study on the effects of differing child-care arrangements on marriages.[5] We mentioned it quickly in chapter 2; here are a few more details. Every father in our study (which included couples that had at least one child under five years old) talked about wanting to be more involved with his children than his own father had been with him. Each father in the study had a full-time job, often a very demanding full-time job. There were simply not enough hours in the week to do everything. Something had to give. Almost every father we spoke with explained that he had lost contact with most of his male friends. These fathers could manage work and family, but not work, family, and friendship. Most (but not all) of them sounded sad about it. Most hoped that it would change as their children got older, but they worried that at least some of their friendships were gone for good. The loss, if it lasted, would be no trivial event in their lives. While women continue to form strong friendships throughout their lives, men tend to rely on old friends. When those old friends are lost, their number of friends declines.[6] These fathers stepped back for the best of reasons. They were busily productive in their careers and had romantic dreams of becoming wonderful husbands and fathers. As far as friends go, however, there is a good chance they found themselves stuck in the left-out predicament, which turns out to be stickier than most of us expect.

Cocooning is not just a trend among parents who want to spend enough time with their children despite their heavy work schedules. It turns out that married couples without children also tend to cocoon. Naomi Gerstel and Natalia Sarkisian studied the period from 1994 to 2004 and found that married couples had fewer ties to relatives than the unmarried and were also less likely to socialize with neighbors or friends.[7] Marriage even seemed to decrease political involvement. And these differences between married and unmarried people existed whether or not the married couples had children. Gerstel and Sarkisian attribute their findings to what they call "the greediness of marriage." Once people get married, they seem to feel relieved of social obligations toward family and friends. Weakening those other ties is probably essential to creating an intimate environment in which a couple can nurture their love, but it may end up closing off another source of nurturance that is equally essential to the long-term health of a marriage.

In an earlier book, *Marriage in Motion*, we worried that there was far too much pressure on a spouse to be everything to his or her partner—best friend, lover, companion, coparent—and that too much reliance on a spouse to meet every social need had become a factor in the high rate of divorce. Our experience in working with many couples and individuals who have struggled to make their marriages last is that a marriage is most likely to flourish when it is woven into a larger tapestry that includes extended family, friends, neighbors, and peers. Without a larger context (and without witnesses, a point we will explore soon), there are few social forces working to keep a couple together, and pure romance can rarely carry the load alone.

Stephanie Coontz, a history professor at Evergreen State College, has similar worries. In her book *Marriage, a History: From Obedience to Intimacy, or How Love Conquered Marriage*, she argues that neglecting other relationships while favoring a spouse as chief confidant places "too many burdens on a fragile institution."[8] She claims that our culture has taken a very unusual turn in its benign view of cocooning, one that would shock people from other eras. "Until a hundred years ago, most societies agreed that it was dangerously antisocial, even pathologically self-absorbed, to elevate marital affection and nuclear-family ties above commitments to neighbors, extended kin, civic duty and religion." It sounds scandalous, and, as Robert Putnam argued powerfully in *Bowling Alone*, it is dangerous behavior that creates serious risks for our democratic institutions. But remember the fathers in our study. They don't sound particularly antisocial. They are each just trying to do a good job at being a father and a worker and a husband. There is precious little time left to do a good job at being a friend and a citizen as well. The majority of mothers in the workforce are in the same bind. Living their lives at a frantic pace, mothers and fathers wish to protect a little time with their spouses and children, and this hardly seems greedy. It may, however, be counterproductive. A married couple floating away together in romantic solitude is an unstable unit. A nuclear family focused inward upon itself is also at risk. Let us look more closely at the fault lines.

The Best Parents in the World

We have all seen our share of heartwarming television shows that end with a child exclaiming, "You're the best parents [or mom, or dad] in the world!" That really is the goal for so many parents today. It is totally understandable that even when both parents are working, they feel an obligation to be there for their children. With so little leisure time, it feels greedy *not* to spend it with the children. Many older mothers already feel guilty that they are spending less time with their children than their own 1950s homemaker mothers spent with them. Many fathers echo the sentiments we have already heard—"I don't want to be absent from my children's lives the way my father was from mine." But people may have overshot the mark. A study by Suzanne Bianchi at the University of Maryland shows that parents today are actually spending *more* time with children than parents did forty years ago.[9] The cost is not only civic engagement and friends. It is also the vitality of the marriage itself. Even the most loving of couples can start to feel slightly estranged when they use up all their leisure time pursuing child-centered activities. Setting the bar high in the parenting area works in direct opposition to the rosy expectations people have of love and marriage when they begin a life together.

We work with many couples who are devoted parents and are still trying to nourish their relationship with each other. A typical couple is William and Carol, who have two young children, Bill (age ten) and Lucy (age eight). On Saturday mornings, the couple split up so that they can each attend one child's soccer game. Then there is a hectic lunch and playdates or birthday parties in the afternoon. Since the two of them find the twelve-dollars-an-hour babysitter fee exorbitant, they often join with another family on Saturday night to have supper together. These suppers turn out to be splendid times for everyone, but the parents are worn out by the time they come home. The children are usually so excited by all the fun that they don't fall asleep until around ten-thirty. Carol has to help Lucy calm down by lying with her in bed in the dark until she falls asleep. Soon Carol is the one who has fallen asleep while Lucy is still quietly talking to herself. William would love to get Carol to come to bed with him for their "date night," but by the time he gets Carol into their own bed, she is dead asleep. He tries not to feel frustrated and wakes up early the next morning, hoping for some sexual activity, but as soon as they wake up, young Bill rushes into their room to ask if he can watch cartoons. With Bill awake, Carol feels too self-conscious to consider making love. Anyway, she says, she's not a morning person, so she doesn't feel very sexual anyway.

William and Carol tell a very familiar story. They love each other deeply, but their high standards about spending time with their children allow very little intimate time with each other. And like most couples, they are too self-conscious to hire a babysitter to keep their children company when they want to make love. So many couples essentially put sexual relationships on ice (not never, but hardly ever) for many years while the children are growing up. William and Carol's story can easily turn into another familiar tale that we hear much too frequently—a couple become estranged from each other while striving to be the best possible parents. Chronic bitterness, an affair, a divorce are all possible outcomes. None of them is in the best interests of the children. As couples' therapists, we are heartbroken when a couple tried so hard to be fantastic parents that they neglected the relationship most essential to their children's emotional health and well-being—their marriage.

Other cultures have other solutions for these problems. Pamela Druckerman, in her book *Lust in Translation: The Rules of Infidelity from Tokyo to Tennessee*, writes that in Japan, married couples frequently stop having sex after the birth of their first child. Husband and wife usually sleep in separate beds, and there is an understanding that husbands may go out to sex clubs without telling their wives about it. Japanese men say, "If you pay for it, it's not cheating." Their wives have another saying—"As long as he's safe, it's good that he's out."[10] In Japanese society, which is extremely child-centered, marriage is preserved by an acceptance of what most Americans would consider to be infidelity. Marriage is also preserved by low romantic expectations for marriage, at least by American standards, a point we will return to later.

The workaholism that we share with Japan provides an important context for "accidentally" falling into an affair. A remarkable statistic from the late psychologist Shirley Glass is that 56 percent of men and 34 percent of women who commit adultery say they were happy with their marriages.[11] In our wonderfully freethinking society people have forgotten the way in which temptation (to use an old-fashioned word) can waylay them into temporarily forgetting their values. Many people spend more time each week with coworkers than with their spouses. With so many hours spent in shared activities with people whom they might find very attractive, it is not at all surprising that sparks sometimes burst into flame. Meanwhile, the spouses are often in the same boat—not meaning to endanger their marriages but simply making friends at work. Modern society may feel light-years away from the iconic 1950s affair between an executive and his secretary, but the same dynamics are alive today.

Even stepping back from friends to have more time with children can backfire. It places more pressure on a spouse, who must then be not only the best friend but the only friend. And that spouse is already overbooked. More surprising, there may be more direct negative effects on child-rearing. A pair of married researchers in California, Philip and Caroline Cowan, ran and systematically evaluated two types of small groups for married couples: one for expectant couples (beginning when the mothers-to-be were six months pregnant) and the other for couples whose first child was about to start elementary school. Each type of group met for only four months, but these brief opportunities for parents to compare notes during stressful times had remarkably positive effects for both parents *and* children. Parents who participated in either type of group were happier in their marriages, more positive about their participation in family life, and had a lower divorce rate over five years. Children whose parents were in the transition-to-school groups did better academically, emotionally, and behaviorally when compared to children whose parents were not in these groups—and these benefits also lasted through the first five years of school.[12] These are remarkable effects for relatively modest interventions. And they suggest that cocooning may be a risky strategy for raising children.

In our offices, we hear couple after couple complain that there is just not enough time for work, children, intimacy with each other, and getting together with friends or relatives. Most often, the friends and relatives get dropped. The irony is that married couples, especially married couples with children, who give up socializing with other adults are at greater risk of losing their sense of proportion about the challenges of married life. So instead these couples end up spending their time (and money) seeing a psychiatrist to restore their perspectives.

The parents' lack of time with other adults also distorts the children's perspectives. Children need their parents' attention, but children also need to know that they cannot *always* have their parents' attention. In their wish to give excellent care to their children, many parents inadvertently mislead their children, giving them the idea that their own wishes are always paramount. Whether they are older parents treating their young children as equals or single parents looking for friendship from their children, many parents describe a moment of exasperation in which they want to yell, "You are not the boss! I am *so* sorry that I ever let you think you were the boss." Even though the GSS tells us spouses remain each other's confidants, we know that too many of their conversations get trumped by children who assume they always get first dibs on their parents' attention. Because their parents seem to agree, children have trouble learning not to interrupt. Often, a couple tells us that they must get a babysitter and leave home to have a real conversation with each other. Teachers throughout the country report that children are much more often bad sports than they used to be and are less aware of the differences between adults and children. Many teachers are especially angry because when they call parents in to discuss a child's behavior, it is no longer unusual for parents to find fault with the teacher rather than go home and try to teach their child to behave better in class. One of the authors is a child psychiatrist and could go on at length about overindulged children whose parents bring them to treatment hoping for biological diagnoses to explain their children's obstreperous behavior. Instead, we will simply say that the importance of being a good sport is emphasized much less in most families than it used to be. Part of the change is the result of cocooning, which, along with smaller family size, reduces the opportunities for children to learn to share the stage with others. It's difficult for children to emerge from this cocoon prepared to step into a world of reciprocal relationships.

An Absence of Witnesses

Another unforeseen consequence of cocooning is the loss of witnesses. Marriages, like all relationships, do far better when they have witnesses. When any aspect of life is seen by others, it feels more real to the participants. The parts of life that are hidden, or simply unobserved by others, start to feel a little split off. When a cocooning spouse is outside of the cocoon, the marriage can seem very far away because it is not interwoven with other relationships. Witnesses also provide a married couple with an audience to perform for *as* a married couple. People try to perform their best for an audience. Some of that improvement lasts after the audience has gone home. We know that sounds bad, but consider cleaning house as an analogy. Most people would tend to let their houses slide into disorder if no one ever came over to visit. Although the slide into messiness may initially be pleasant, soon the clutter gets out of hand and even the thought of trying to clean up becomes overwhelming. In the same way, if there are never any witnesses to our dealings with spouses or children, we are just a little less likely to take excellent care of them. It is embarrassing to admit it, but most people we talk to respond with rueful smiles of recognition. Each of us has his or her own slightly embarrassing memories of behaving less well when no one is watching, and the loss of witnesses is not a trivial development for family life. Social isolation is a common denominator among most families in which child abuse occurs.[13]

There is a fair amount of overlap between the witness function and the comparing-notes function of friends and relatives. The most effective witnesses are not those who judge and scold from a position of superiority, but those who watch and speak from a shared experience or the memory of a shared experience; friends and relatives who add perspective on a couple's ordinary human strivings and ordinary human failings in living with a spouse or raising children. When nuclear families turn inward, parents are much more likely to lose perspective, get too upset about little things, and stop being able to view themselves, each other, and their children in reasonable ways.

In writing about marriage, we have described a sort of tidal ebb and flow of closeness in even the best of relationships. Even when people are extremely close to each other with a strong romantic connection, they tend to drift apart regularly, at least a little, while each goes about his or her separate business in the world. The security of a good relationship in fact allows for greater freedom and creativity in the world—as long as both partners are reasonably confident that they will turn back toward each other again and re-store their closeness. That confidence is hard to come by these days, since so many people have not grown up with firsthand experience of what a healthy marriage looks like when it lasts. Without that understanding, people experiencing these inevitable drifts can misinterpret them as catastrophic signs. The more dismal a child's experience of his or her parents' relationship, the more the child is likely to invent a script for how a loving relationship *ought* to look, usually from whole cloth with a little help from movies, books, and television. The less experience with real-life happy marriages that a child has, the more the script looks like a romantic fairy tale. The more unrealistic the script, the more the child grows up to constantly find fault with how any real relationship actually *is*. Many marriages that are simply experiencing the usual vicissitudes of warmth and coolness die premature deaths because when real life departs from the Hollywood scripts, people think "the bells aren't ringing anymore" and start planning their exit strategies.

That is just the moment when the commentary of witnesses and the perspective of friends can make an immense difference. By talking frankly with friends who are also in real relationships, with their peaks and valleys and shifts over time, friends (and relatives) can support each other during the down times and allow a marriage to regain its balance. The sociologist Stacey Oliver, in a book called *Best Friends and Marriage*, writes eloquently about how a woman's close friends can form a bastion of support when she is feeling doubts about her marriage by providing both perspective and practical advice.

However, Oliker studied women's friendships in the 1980s. These days, when women are likely to remain single for much longer, it may not be as easy to find a group of women who want to support the marriages of friends, especially when they don't have partners themselves. We hear new mothers tell us that they have trouble finding other new mothers with whom they can go to the park, and new wives tell us that they have trouble finding young wives to talk to about married life. In addition, many women and men are now very private about their marriages for fear of betraying their "best friend." As psychiatrists, we often encounter people who feel they can only discuss their marriages with a paid confidant sworn to confidentiality, and then only in order to get perspective on their marriages. Allowing witnesses to one's marriage feels more like a betrayal of a spouse's trust than it once did, tightening the cocoon and reducing an important check on unrestrained and unrealistic romantic visions of what a marriage should be.

Our High Expectations of Love and Marriage

Unrealistic romantic visions, like the high bars that we set for parent-child relationships, are another factor in our increasing isolation. They lead some people to give up too soon. They lead some people to not try at all. We have seen fundamentally healthy relationships shatter under the stress of an overintense scrutiny of ordinary disappointments and passing rough spots. We have heard many young people point to the high divorce rate as an obvious reason never to marry. There is a circular interaction between a rising standard for a good-enough marriage and the rising divorce rate—each drives the other higher and, in turn, is driven higher. We as a nation are both deeply skeptical about marriage and incurably romantic. Paradoxically, each viewpoint fuels the other. How else to explain the high rate of remarriage after divorce and the high rate of divorce after remarriage?

The average marriage today *is* better than the average marriage in 1920s Middletown. Spouses *do* talk to each other. They even talk to each other about important matters. We want so much more. We expect so much more. Most people feel entitled to a marriage that is, at almost every moment, a fulfilling relationship. Neither party is ever supposed to be unfaithful, lie, hold back, or even slack off in his or her energetic efforts to keep romance alive. (One result is the "relationship talk," dreaded by many husbands, in which a wife will explain the ways in which her needs are not being met.) Each partner is expected to earn money and to participate fully on the domestic front. Time for outside friendships is diminished. Spouses are supposed to be both best friends who offer conversation from the heart and passionate lovers who surprise each other with romantic seductions. They must not flinch or stumble when they are called upon to shift gears between those two roles at the drop of a hat. Like a hat trick in hockey, pulling it off deserves to be celebrated, but we can't expect to see it happen every night, especially when the rhythm of daily life is so frenetic that there is precious little time for debriefing and relaxing between role transitions. It's a wonder how many marriages *do* last!

A punishing rise in expectations for marriage has also been described by sociologists David Popenoe and Barbara Dafoe Whitehead: "From the mid-60s on, the affectional requirements for marriage ratcheted upward, the demands for emotional satisfactions in family life escalated, the pursuit of love connections took on a manic intensity. Marital happiness, like the definition of a good provider, turned out to be a highly elastic notion."[14]

They also connect these rising expectations with a "substantial weakening of the institution of marriage." The consequences for the country of that weakening have been vigorously debated; we simply want to underline its relationship to loneliness. Peter Bearman and Paolo Parigi from Columbia University looked carefully at data from the North Carolina Poll, an annual representative survey of adults in North Carolina. They were interested in the "silent" subgroup in the GSS survey, the ones who reported that they had not discussed anything important with anybody over the previous six months. Those individuals were more likely to be nonwhite or not married (that is, never married or currently divorced).[15] Singleness is a risk factor for silence. It does not damn one to silence and social isolation; it just increases the odds. It might also simply be a marker for social incompetence, which could be an underlying reason for an unmarried state. That argument becomes a little less convincing these days, however, when half of the adults in the country are unmarried.

Many single adults are certainly tied to rich social networks. Recent books like *The New Single Woman* show how single women over thirty-five are living engaged and fulfilling lives, with networks of friends providing most of the joys of companionship that were once thought to be found only in marriage. Some of the celebration is very much about the discovery of an alternative route that skirts the impossibly high bar for a good marriage: "Knowing that you are not dependent on one crucial other to bring intimacy into your life can be a tremendous relief. It can diminish self-judgment and self-blame. It can allow life to be lived first hand rather than in a waiting pattern."[16]

When one of the authors was a resident in psychiatry, a patient attempted suicide after a breakup with his lover. A wise supervisor offered some simple advice: "Tell that young man not to put all his eggs in one basket." Those words may have been our earliest instruction in the importance of social networks. For the average person, however, developing and sustaining a social network is an easier task with a partner. That is where psychiatrists and other therapists can step in—as a partner in the enterprise when no one else is available—but spouses have also traditionally done a good job.

It is interesting to place Bearman and Parigi's report next to the census data on the dramatic sixty-year rise in the percentage of one-person households. It is easier to be single these days. There is less social stigma attached to it, less that needs to be explained. Old Maid is no longer a popular game, and the social stereotyping that it represents is largely gone. With rising prosperity, it is also much easier for a single person to live alone, to set up a household that is clearly and decisively his or her own. It is also one more way in which following an apparently straight path to greater contentment can get lead someone into a trap.

Our culture's idealistic notions about love, which at first blush seem harmless and even sweet, can throw people off track in their search for partners. So many people are intimidated by the high bar. They often have trouble finding examples of couples who embody the blissful state that they desire. They prepare for lives of singlehood, just in case, and these become the lives they both fear and expect, even if they marry in the short run. It is no longer fashionable to suppress one's own wishes for the sake of the spouse, family, extended family, or community. (The current idealization of love tends to play down self-sacrifice for love's sake.) Unfortunately, the mix of very high hopes for marriage and the fear that any particular relationship will not last means that many young people get set in their ways while they wait longer to get married (if they marry at all). They become rigid in their own preferences and opinions. They define small matters of taste as central to their identities. The need to keep limber and somewhat adaptable so that one can share living space with family and friends is no longer the requirement it once was. Women are proud not to be "pleasers" after their journeys of self-discovery. Men who try to please risk being called wusses or wimps. We as a culture admire the person who can live alone and have things *just so*—a small key to our nation's profligacy with the world's resources. Decorating a little abode with knickknacks that represent one's identity gets transformed from self-indulgence to self-definition. People seek partners who will fit seamlessly into the lives they have already created.

A Stitch in the Social Fabric

In 2006, the American Community Survey made national headlines with the news that married couples, with or without children, made up less than half of the nation's households. As a *New York*

Times headline writer put it, "To Be Married Means to Be Out-numbered."[17] While there may be more than a bit of age-appropriate bravado shaping their responses, in 2007, less than a third of girls in their senior year of high school reported believing that marriage was an essential element in a well-lived life or a well-functioning community.[18] This sea change in attitude is power-fully liberating, but if carried too far, it holds significant risks. We have already described some of the reasons for the change: The bar for contentment in marriage keeps rising. The bar for good parenting keeps rising. The landscape around is scattered with broken families. It is hard to spot real-life examples of happily married parents. It is much easier to find couples who seem to be driving themselves crazy with work and parenting. Who wouldn't hope to find a better idea? Why should we be surprised that many college students in our practice say "I don't have time for a rela-tionship," even though we know that for most people, the truth is likely to be "If I were in a relationship, I would be able to do so much more"?

There are other things that we know about marriage. We know that marriage, like other important social connections, im-proves health and longevity. Marriage, like other important social connections, improves emotional health and resilience. (In chap-ters 8 and 9, we will consider these important effects of social sup-port further.) Marriage, like other partnerships, can transform a daunting enterprise (like raising children) from unimaginable to merely challenging. Marriage may at times absorb energy from other pursuits; it can also free energy for other pursuits by resolv-ing the uncertainties about loving and being loved that are often so all-consuming during adolescence and beyond.

We know that marriage is a very peculiar relationship, with a blend of freedom and constraint, friendship and kinship, that is unlike any other. We are free to choose spouses as we might choose our friends, but we are not free to leave our spouses as we might leave our friends. A marriage may be ended, but not casually and not without the formal assent of others. Marriage (at least since the Reformation in Western society) requires witnesses. It can begin only with a public vow, and it can end only with a public revocation of that vow. We live in interesting times. Gay couples, who in most places have not been allowed that public vow, are fighting for the right to have it. Heterosexual couples, who have long been expected to make that public vow, are increasingly choosing to do without it.

What would be lost if marriage bit the dust? Or became an archaic formalism chosen by only a few? We believe that a vital component of a strong social fabric would be lost. Marriage may be greedy, but it is also generative in ways that create engagement in larger communities. Marriage is perhaps the most important way that human beings keep loneliness at bay, even if it is not the only answer or the whole answer. Marriage allows a degree of confidence in the future of a relationship, not an ironclad guarantee but an explicit shared determination to try and make it through the rough patches that are inevitable in all relationships. Without that public vow, it is much harder to withstand the lure of a lazy pessimism, a casual "What's the use?," or an enticing stranger. As we wrote in an earlier discussion of marriage vows, "Lacking an overt promise, it is much harder for a couple to weather the changes that happen in a close relationship over time. If one person notices the other emotionally wandering, there is no mutual agreement to do something about it in order to prolong the relationship. Drift is far more threatening; it is seen as foreshadowing an exit rather than an effort at renewal."[19] If someone has grown up with divorced parents, close relationships are even more fraught. They are haunted by fears of dissolution. A person who has not seen a relationship weather the difficult times is a little more likely to panic and take flight in moments of anger, disillusionment, or estrangement. The obstacles to immediate flight that marriage imposes create at least a few more opportunities to regain perspective. We don't mean to imply that divorce is never the right decision. We just don't want couples to startle too easily at the ordinary ups and downs of a shared life—which brings us back to the rewards and risks of cocooning.

Resilient marriages usually achieve a balance between restorative intimacy and outward-looking engagement; the couple is alternately a self-contained unit and a building block in a larger social network. Couples, especially couples with children, need to remember the importance of spending time with friends, both as individuals and as couples, to be able to compare notes, to regain perspective, and simply to keep the world from feeling too small and stifling. Parents need to model balancing family and friendship for their children, as well as teach children the skills of friendship (which include initiating get-togethers instead of counting on arranged playdates). These points may seem self-evident and trivial, but some of the most striking data that Robert Putnam presents in *Bowling Alone* documents a rapid decline over recent decades in people having friends over to their homes *and* in their going out to see friends. In Putnam's words, "Visits with friends are now on the social capital endangered species list."[20] While the reason for staying home, holed up with spouse and children, may be partly a desire to breathe life into a marriage, over time its effect can be to drain the life out of a marriage.

Children also have a changed view of their parents' marriage, even when the marriage lasts. It is a more restricted view. Because of the complex schedules of many two-working-parent families, children see more of each parent separately but less of their parents interacting together. What is lost is an opportunity to learn about marriage relationships by direct observation. It is also harder for children to figure out whether their parents are happy with each other. Combine that with a superstitious fear of advertising a happy marriage when divorce rates are so high, and we create a cohort of children who have nothing beyond divorce statistics and the media to shape their understanding of marriage. Paradoxically, at a time when the average marriage may be happier than it has been through most of human history, there is a relative vacuum of eloquence about the wonderful aspects of marriage when it does succeed.

In summary, ideas of love and marriage have changed over the last century. People's expectations of a "good marriage" have soared, while fears about divorce have made them much more skittish. Parents' time with children has increased, along with parents' anxiety about their children. Time for couples to be alone together has greatly diminished. Both parents tend to work harder at paid jobs than their counterparts did during the decades after World War II, but increased time at work has not reduced the importance placed on having a very satisfying personal life. Most couples now socialize less with family and friends and, consequently, receive less support from a wider social network. Add in current economic insecurities, and the idea of embarking on a marriage, especially a marriage with children, becomes very intimidating. The reluctance that so many young people express about getting married is completely understandable. The standards for a good marriage seem hopelessly high, and real-life couples often seem frantic and confused. Who would not be skeptical or even terrified about the odds of making a good marriage? People are faced with high aspirations gone awry. Their rising expectations about love and marriage turn out to be one more element that is fueling what appears to be an inexorable march toward more and more people living alone.

CHAPTER 8

The Ripple Effects of Increasing Social Isolation

The movement in our country toward greater social isolation is subtle. It is especially easy to miss in everyday life because we, as a people, try to let others live their own lives. We don't believe that we are our brothers' keepers. If neighbors seem to have dis-appeared into their houses or apartments, we treat it as their own business. Who are we to interfere? None of us wants to be the kind of person who is judgmental and arrogant about his or her own choices. We try hard not to signal that we see our neighbors' drift into social isolation as a bit peculiar, if not downright depressing. And besides, when we each are feeling isolated ourselves, there is comfort in knowing that we are not the only ones.

In this chapter, we will look at the long-term consequences for individuals and for the larger society of this drift apart. These con-sequences are far-reaching and, as we have begun to see, often at odds with the goals that people have in mind when they step back from the fray. A perpetual theme in cautionary tales, both old and new, is "be careful what you wish for." Almost everyone wants to be happier. These days, that wish most often translates into efforts to reduce a sense of being too busy, perpetually on call, and con-stantly pushed around by the demands of others. As people step back from their engagement with others and shed some of their obligations toward their communities, they expect to experience a glorious sense of personal freedom, a liberation of energy that can now be focused more precisely on just those activities that they think will bring them true satisfaction. Yet when those same obligations toward others are fulfilled, they can lead to feelings of satisfaction, connection, and meaning (along with less guilt) that can also liberate creative energies. As we'll see, the range of effects that social connectedness (and social isolation) has on a person's well-being is remarkably broad.

Social Isolation and Physical Health

Social support is an important and independent determinant of overall health. The degree of social connection has significant effects on longevity, on an individual's response to stress, on the robustness of immune functions, and on the incidence and course of a variety of specific illnesses. In diseases as varied as heart attacks and dementia, medical research has repeatedly found that social networks and social activity have a protective effect. Isolated individuals are nearly twice as likely to die in a ten-year period as their more socially involved neighbors. That increase in mortality is above and beyond the effects of the bad lifestyle choices that are more common with social isolation, such as smoking, lack of exercise, poor diet, and obesity. Social connection itself appears to have direct effects on human biology.[1] A report from the 2003 Dahlem Workshop on Attachment and Bonding offers a succinct summary of a vast body of research: "Positive social relationships are second only to genetics in predicting health and longevity in humans."[2]

A new study adds a dramatic piece to the puzzle. Subjective social isolation (more simply described as loneliness) alters the expression of more than two hundred genes that control immune response.[3] Steve Cole, the lead author of the study, offers his own commentary on it: "What this shows us is the biological impact of social isolation reaches down into some of our most important basic internal processes—the activity of our genes."[4]

Social Isolation and Civic Health

Robert Putnam's work on social capital (a measure of the strength and extensiveness of social ties) and civic engagement has received enough attention that there is no need to repeat his arguments here. We will simply note that he offers the political equivalent of the medical conclusion that strong social connections are necessary for a healthy organism. Before turning his attention to social capital in the United States, Putnam conducted a detailed analysis of civic life and regional governments in Italy. In his conclusion, Putnam wrote, "For political stability, for government effectiveness, and even for economic progress, social capital may be even more important than physical or human capital."[5] Those words explain Putnam's urgent concern about the evidence for decreasing social capital in America that he presented in *Bowling Alone*. Looking at data from the United States, he concluded that there is a strong correlation between measures of social capital and child well-being, effective schools, neighborhood safety, economic efficiency, and effective government. These are ripples our country ignores at its peril.

Social Isolation and Global Health

In chapter 5, we explored the ecological consequences of the steady rise in one-person households in this country and in Europe. There are ecological consequences to social isolation even when people are not living alone. In our consumer-oriented culture, a common solution to not having enough people in one's life is to turn to things, objects that are "just right," objects that will define one's identity through possessions rather than through one's place in a social world. Consumers' quests for self-definition drives our economy. That is the good news. Consumers' quests for self-definition also increases our global ecological footprint. That is the bad news. But there is a paradox at the heart of the quest. The explosion of consumer choices that allows purchases to become acts of self-definition may also leave people less happy.

In his book *The Paradox of Choice*, Barry Schwartz presents important research that points to a surprising conclusion: an abundance of choices decreases rather than increases happiness. Most people reasonably assume that when they have a wider range of choices, they are better able to choose what they really want and are more likely to be happy. The assumption turns out to be right only when a person goes from having no choice at all to having a small number of choices. The problems come when the number of choices goes from a few to many. When people have *lots* of choices, they worry more about making the wrong choices. That worry trumps the joyful sense of freedom. Our family version of Barry Schwartz's discovery occurred when we took our young children into an ice cream store that had dozens of flavors and at least a dozen more toppings to choose from. The look in the children's eyes quickly changed from delight to worry as they surveyed the mind-numbing options. By the time most people thoroughly investigate all the choices available to them, desire itself often fades away. And if a choice is made, the reality of the object, once possessed, seems oddly disappointing. Which leads to us to another of Barry Schwartz's conclusions: not only does having a large number of possible choices leave people less happy, it also does not even usually lead to better decisions. Schwartz's work is important because it teaches us something that we somehow continue not to learn from our own experiences with overabundant choice. Common sense tells us that having more choices is better than having less. Science contradicts that. Yet most people stick with common sense. They welcome opportunities to expand their choices. Indefatigably, they continue their quests for the perfect purchases that will help define who they are and offer "good company" in somewhat lonely lives.

Another version of the paradox of choice was described by James Surowiecki in *The New Yorker*.[6] Many companies report that customers buy gadgets that have more built-in options than they will ever use. This pressure toward greater complexity is sometimes called "feature creep." Complex gadgets sell well. Then, once the gadget is home, buyers discover that they would have preferred something simpler and easier to figure out. Companies often get calls from bewildered customers who think their new cameras (to choose one common example) don't quite work, when the problem really is that the camera's multiple functions are too complex for the average buyer. Companies that design (and sell) consumer products face their own paradox. They can build in extra options that will befuddle buyers, or they can offer stripped-down, streamlined products that few will buy because most people *believe* they will be happier with more choices.

A song by the popular singer-songwriter Nanci Griffith has a rousing refrain that celebrates the car radio as the perfect antidote for heartbreak and loneliness. Many who drove cars across this big country in the late twentieth century know the feeling. But now, when you can't find a friend, you've got so much more than an AM radio. You have a DVD player that will let you watch movies or favorite television shows wherever you are. You have a BlackBerry or iPhone that will get you on the Internet and even let you browse for other gadgets to keep you company. You have a home entertainment center that can completely distract you from the fact that there is no one to invite over to your home. Pretty soon, you feel on the verge of complete self-sufficiency, *almost* free from those bothersome twinges of loneliness that can break through during an inconvenient pause in the entertainment.

America's economy now depends on the quest for the perfectly fulfilling purchase. Henry Ford invented the five-day workweek so that his workers could become consumers on the weekends. Without a weekend, he surmised, people would have no time to spend the money they earned in his factory on the cars that they manufactured and no time to drive the cars.[7] But in those days, the image of the car was as much about family togetherness (the traditional Sunday drive) as it was about solitary escape. Now, cars, like so many other possessions that were once shared, are for individuals. Along with increasing affluence and the wish for consumer goods to reflect one's particular personality and taste, there is the growing trend in America not to share one's particular belongings with anyone. Parents with more than one child are likely to get several of the most coveted toys so their children won't have to share them. Parents sometimes sum up this approach by saying, "I have three only children!" The explicit goal is to avoid sibling rivalry. Often it is also a well-intentioned effort to be fair to every child. With certain toys, like a bicycle that needs to be sized for the particular child, this approach makes perfect sense, but if we are talking about a personal computer or television or even a video game system, children who do not learn to share from an early age are likely to be reluctant sharers throughout their lives. They will not see this as selfish. They are likely to see it as an issue of fairness and self-expression. Problems hit when these children are forced to share rooms in college, and again when they consider marrying or try to make a marriage work. Problems also hit when sharing is proposed to them as a way of reducing individual contributions to global warming. Americans' aversion to car pools is, after all, just a particular example of the antipathy to sharing.

As any parent knows, the wish not to share grows easily into a wish to have *more* than one's share. Excessive solitude both fuels that wish and allows it freer expression. Especially when material goods are used as a substitute for human connection, a constant flow of new possessions is required to keep wistfulness at bay. Last year in New York City, we passed an elegant store whose name summed up the problem: More and More. We watched the store from across the street, keeping a safe distance.

The More We Stay In, the More We Live in a Frightening World

We turn now to several less obvious consequences of increasing social isolation. We begin with two worrisome effects of cocooning, which, as we've noted, is the family version of social isolation. The first effect is excessive fears about a child's physical and mental health, which can lead to unnecessary (and potentially harmful) interventions. The second is excessive fears about a child's safety in the world, which can breed a child who mirrors the parents' dread.

One consequence of cocooning—families living on their own without friends, relatives, and neighbors who drop by—is a large cohort of overscrutinizing parents raising overscrutinized children. Young children are already watching their parents very closely to know how they (the children) are doing. Parents who are also nervously watching, searching for the smallest sign that all is not going well with a child's development and always ready to sound the alarm, are likely to raise anxious children with a wide range of mysterious symptoms that seem to cry out for diagnoses. This nervous watching, with no one to help isolated parents gain perspective on their fears, may be partially responsible for the fact that more American children and adolescents are on psychoactive medications than ever before.[8]

When parents sense that their child is falling behind educationally, socially, or in some other way, they start to feel a sense of despair, a vertiginous panic that they, as parents, may have lost the whole ball game. Meanwhile, the child can be quite spooked to find his or her parents looking so scared about something that the child had hoped was just a small matter. Soon a cascade of anxiety is rippling from parents to child and back again, gaining strength along the way. These tremendous struggles and tension around ordinary stumbles in a child's development often end with parents or teachers sending the child for a psychological evaluation. As psychiatrists, we must admit that we are hard-pressed to send a child away with no diagnosis at all. These days, even if we try to reassure parents that all is well, their response is more likely to be doctor-shopping than relief. After all, parents who read almost daily about the prevalence of biological disorders and the wonders of medication feel irresponsible if they leave any stone unturned while investigating ways to smooth their child's path to maturity and success. If psychiatrists working with parents turn over enough stones, they can usually uncover what is sometimes called a subclinical condition—a pattern of symptoms that falls short of a specific diagnosable illness but seems to lean in its direction. When both parents and teachers want a diagnosis and treatment badly enough, a psychiatrist is more likely to grant a subclinical condition the status of a formal diagnosis. The child has an illness and requires specialized treatment. The attention shifts from the behavior patterns that many children share to a child's particular primary diagnosis, and from ordinary ways to teach *all* children how to persevere in the face of challenges and discouragement to diagnosis-specific treatment. What falls by the wayside is something we discussed in the previous chapter—comparing notes with friends, relatives, and other parents, which is probably the best way for parents themselves to persevere in the face of the inevitable challenges and discouragements of parenting, a way to grab hold of something solid before panic takes over completely.

Parents who don't have relatives or friends to help them gain perspective on their own offspring are more likely to overgeneralize from the strange, quirky symptoms that are part and parcel of normal child development and to start wondering if their child will grow up to be a strange, quirky, and abnormal adult. These fears can often be eased quickly by an in-depth talk with an experienced parent, but these days the best-parent status seems to belong to the parents who get psychiatric or psychological evaluations for their ever-so-slightly quirky children (along with special school privileges like extra time on exams). The evaluation offers parents the opportunity to discuss the details of their child's development with a professional instead of with grandmothers and friends, but the result is often a treatment plan rather than an encouraging perspective on how many variations there are to normal development. And, of course, once enough children in a community are in treatment, the very occasional comparing of notes that still goes on among parents is likely to lead directly to a child psychologist's or psychiatrist's office.

We do see an occasional brave parent (most often it is a father) who proclaims that he was just like the child when he was a boy and look how well he turned out. The mother usually has a very hard time quieting her fears with that one lone voice. And besides, a mother often has plenty to say about how Dad turned out, whatever his own views on the subject might be. A worried parent can usually trump a reassuring one, especially in the middle of the night and when there is no one else to talk to. So parents continue to worry, and children continue to acquire one strange habit after another, partly just to test whether their parents will look even more worried, and partly because they're still hoping to find something reassuring in their parents' response. A little less cocooning could help turn things around.

Fears about a child's physical safety are just as alarming as fears about a child's development, and here too cocooning acts as an unhealthy amplifier. Most parents are more concerned than ever before about the dangers that can befall elementary-school children who are allowed to walk around the neighborhood alone. Even in rather safe communities, a ten- or eleven-year-old is regularly walked a block or two to a friend's house rather than sent out the door alone. The trend is even more surprising in the face of a general improvement in national crime statistics.[9]

When parents feel disconnected from the surrounding community, their imaginations are more likely to run wild in the streets, picturing all sorts of terrible fates that could befall their beloved children in a neighborhood that the parents don't know very well themselves. The evening news does not help one bit, with its usual focus on murders, abductions, and sexual molestations. Certainly there are dangers in the world. Certainly any loving parent will worry at least some of the time. But curiously, when parents are able to make homes for their families in affluent communities, often explicitly to offer their children safe and idyllic childhoods, their worries about the physical safety of their children do not reliably quiet down. Part of the reason is that affluent suburbs are often communities of near-strangers, where neighbors' houses (and neighbors themselves) do not spoil the idyllic view, leaving families feeling both disconnected and vulnerable. No comforting network of watchful eyes shares the burden of worry. And most affluent suburban parents never take certain commonsense measures that a self-reliant *Little House on the Prairie* family would have considered an obvious mix of hospitality and precaution. When every family understood the fragility of their lives, they made it their business to know the neighbors over a wide area. Interdependence was made explicit. Neighbors were expected to watch out for one another. Neighbors were expected to know one another.

It is well known that when social isolation increases, child abuse tends to increase; or, to put it differently, child-abusing parents are much more likely to be socially isolated than non-child-abusing parents.[10] Often the angriest parents live in isolation. And angry parents tend to project their anger onto their neighbors without the reality check that spending time with neighbors provides. Parents who see little of their neighbors are likely to imagine neighbors who are just as irritable and desperate as they are themselves, especially if a parent is feeling overwhelmed and alone with child-rearing. So it really isn't so surprising that isolated parents worry about letting their children walk freely in the neighborhood without supervision. Whether we look at people in rural areas who guard their constitutional right to have weapons for self-protection or prosperous families who feel they have to fence out the world for peace of mind, it seems that the farther one goes from other people, the more worrisome and hostile one imagines those other people to be.

The Dangerous Book for Boys recently became a bestseller because so many parents feel nostalgic for the old days when children went out to play, roaming the woods or the neighborhood, instead of staying indoors with the electronic entertainment of the moment. A study of American children's relationships to nature offers a no longer startling fact: "In contrast to the hours spent per child per week in front of electronic entertainment, children living in the United States reportedly spend on average only thirty minutes of unstructured time outdoors each week."[11] That fact may not be surprising, but some of the authors' other conclusions certainly are: "Outdoor play and nature experience has proven beneficial for cognitive functioning, reduction in symptoms of ADD, increase in self-discipline, and emotional well-being at all developmental stages." Even without this new information, many parents are already longing for what felt like safer times, when children were allowed to experiment and play outdoors in more exciting ways. Overscrutinizing parents who want to swing the pendulum back can now provide books of instruction for their children on how to pursue slightly reckless activities. These are the same activities that children used to discover for themselves. Unfortunately, it is not quite the same when their parents provide them with the instruction manual. The play activities felt exciting *because* it was understood that parents would disapprove of them. Children also need some unsupervised time to experiment in both thought and action in order to form their own identities. Without alone time to think and to explore, children grow up without much sense of what they think about the world. Paradoxically, the isolation of cocooning reduces a child's opportunity to explore the world alone.

We don't mean to oversimplify a parent's predicament. The word *cocooning* suggests isolation as a luxury. Isolation can also be a response to danger, real or imagined. Just as social isolation can increase fears, fears can increase social isolation. Certainly, that is true in the most dangerous neighborhoods. Sadly, fear and the move toward greater social isolation can also be a consequence of neighborhood diversity. In work done since *Bowling Alone*, Robert Putnam compared homogeneous neighborhoods with more diversified neighborhoods, where people of many different ethnic backgrounds live cheek by jowl with one another. His troubling conclusion: the more diversified the neighborhood, the more intergroup hostility (hostility between groups) *and* intragroup hostility (hostility within groups) increase. In other words, if (for example) Caucasians, African Americans, and Asians are integrated into a city neighborhood, their hostility both toward one another and toward their "own kind" will increase. As Putnam wrote in 2007, "Diversity seems to trigger not in-group/out-group division but anomie or social isolation...In colloquial language, people living in ethnically diverse settings appear to hunker down—that is, to pull in like a turtle."[12]

Maybe we should just admit that in a large, diversified country such as the United States, tension is always higher than in more homogeneous countries. David Brooks made that argument writing about Iraq in the *New York Times*, with a nod to our evolutionary fear of strangers.[13] In the short run (and maybe the not-so-short run), melting pots stir up a lot of nervous irritability—along with the American habit of an easy smile. In a nation of potentially hostile others, a quick smile just to let someone know that you mean no harm serves an important function. The hostility of diverse neighborhoods runs counter to the American dream, but it has certainly been the experience of vast numbers of immigrant groups trying to make new homes in vibrant and tumultuous cities.

Attempts to create racial balance in Harvard dormitories over recent decades has led to the same conclusion. When groups of students could choose their houses (as Harvard dorms are known), they chose to live with students of similar background. Soon they had effectively created specific houses for students of color, houses that were highly sought out. The college administration, disturbed by the disappearance of diversity in college housing, moved from choice to random assignment. The pattern chosen by the students themselves, however, reflected their own experiences of the phenomenon that Putnam describes. We should probably add that Putnam himself is not so discouraged by his own data. He looks hopefully at American history and concludes that, in the long run, many differences (like interfaith marriages) that used to cause so much distress have gradually become less divisive.

Putnam's work on neighborhood diversity and aggression must be put alongside another ripple effect that we examined in chapter 4—even seemingly trivial experiences of social exclusion lead to an increase in aggressive behavior. Those experiences are more likely to be built into everyday life in diverse neighborhoods. The effect is neatly summed up by the title of a research report: "If You Can't Join Them, Beat Them: Effects of Social Exclusion on Aggressive Behavior."[14] Putnam's study may be a naturalistic version of the laboratory experiments on social exclusion. There is a convergence of epidemiological data linking breakdowns in social connection with increases in crime. In 1994, David Lester found that "statistics measuring decreasing social integration (e.g., divorce, declining marriage and birth rates) showed a nearly perfect correlation with homicide rates."[15] Other studies confirm that criminal, violent, and antisocial behavior have increased as people have chosen to live alone more often and to divorce more often. As epidemiologists remind us, correlation is not proof of cause, but Jean Twenge and Roy Baumeister (the researchers whose work on social exclusion we cited) are convinced that social exclusion leads to increased aggression, rather than the other way around. Their hypothesis is that aggressive impulses are normally held in check by social relationships and community norms—constraints that we usually refer to as a moral sense or conscience. When a person loses the sense of belonging to a community, these impulses are less likely to be restrained.[16] (Remember our discussion of the importance of witnesses in the previous chapter.) So our notion that feeling left out can lead to a sense of paranoia and hostility seems to be borne out by recent research. Both an increase in irrational fears of the world out there and an increase in the actual danger and aggression in the world out there are, at least in part, the consequences of increased social isolation.

The Loss of Parents' and Teachers' Authority

If we continue our focus on modern parenting (which includes both single parents and coupled parents), we can see another dramatic consequence of social isolation. The more parents are isolated from everyone except their children, the more parents inadvertently rely upon their children for companionship. Parents' social isolation often feels imposed, but, as we discussed in the previous chapter, there is usually a complex mix of constraints and choices. Parents (especially single parents) have difficulty raising and providing for their children with time left over for socializing with friends, but parents are also constantly making choices based on what they believe is most important. The effects on their children are complex. When a parent's longing for companionship is focused on a child, somewhere along the way, the parent may lose the authority needed to shape or discipline the child. When a child is a parent's primary confidant (what is sometimes called a *parenti-fied child*), the child begins to feel like an equal, an adult equivalent. Frequently, that child will make clear to a parent that he or she will not obey just because the parent is an adult who is responsible for the child's support and well-being. These children demand to be consulted as equals. And the predilection for *not* obeying "just be-cause" may emerge at school as a parallel difficulty in accepting in-struction that, at least some of the time, *does* depend on obeying an authority figure.

In the Massachusetts General Hospital child psychiatry clinic, we see many excellent single parents, frequently mothers, who confide in their children rather than other adults. Another sign of the children's status as equals (at least in the eyes of the children themselves) is their regularly being taken into their mothers' beds for reassurance when they are seized by nighttime fears. Later, when the children are oppositional about their mothers' rules for the household, we find ourselves in the ticklish position of fight-ing against a well-established family culture. The children's view is that they are treated fairly (meaning as equals) some of the time, and outrageously unfairly (meaning like children) at other times, simply because the rules for parent and child are not exactly the same. The parents are also frequently bewildered. Why are they unable to exert effective authority with their children? The child must have a problem, and the search for a psychiatric diagnosis be-gins. The child, of course, does have a problem. The shift from being treated as an equal to being told to obey "just because" a parent may know better is extremely difficult for a young child to comprehend. Even the best-intentioned and most loving parents have trouble explaining that shift to their children.

We have found that as some of these children get older, they insist that their parents have to earn the right to be obeyed, often by being present for the children more of the time. Here, the dif-ficulty has more to do with the problem of overextended parents, which is itself a cause of social isolation, rather than the resulting social isolation itself. The children are keeping mental accounts. They have a strong sense of fairness about how the numbers add up. Sufficient time spent with the children or working directly on the children's behalf is an essential requirement for those children's obedience. And there is a confusing mix of merit and excuse in a child's claim that a parent who has been shrugging off parental duties need not be obeyed.

Parents are not the only people reeling from the difficulties of exerting authority over children. Teachers have an even more difficult problem with a child's predilection to think, "I am the boss of myself." Just getting children to sit still and listen to the teacher is much harder than it used to be. The problem is not only in the hardwiring of children with attention deficit disorder. Part of the problem is that many children have come believe that no adult should ever expect them to do something that they have not decided to do themselves. In particular, they have developed a deep conviction that it is unfair to be told to do anything "boring." As much as we all wish to make learning exciting for children, there are times when the development of any skill or understanding will be boring. A tolerance for moments of boredom in any enterprise is actually an essential skill that all children were once expected to learn in the classrooms of even the most inspiring teachers. The change in parent-child relationships that goes along with increasing social isolation makes teaching that skill even harder. Parents, teachers, and clinicians are often surprised to find that even children with severe attentional problems can pay attention rather well when they are doing something that they are in the mood to do.

Children who believe they need not take instruction from adults because they are already adult-equivalents themselves become very difficult to teach. A child's natural difficulty with self-discipline (which is a hardwiring issue related to the immaturity of a child's central nervous system) is compounded by an unwillingness to let adults help with self-discipline. *And why*, the child thinks, *should self-discipline be necessary anyway?* When children are accustomed to thinking of themselves as adult-equivalents, they certainly don't understand why learning should require work and difficulty. After all, their parents seem competent without having to spend the days in school or the nights with boring homework.

These difficulties in school spawn a whole set of social problems that have been well described by sociologists. Large national studies have shown that children who are not well connected to their schools are much more at risk for delinquency, early pregnancy, substance abuse, and suicidality.[17] One of the major reasons that children end up disconnected from their schools is their experience of academic failure. And, as if these social ills are not enough of a burden, there is also evidence that early difficulties in school increase the risk of physical illness and early death. Specifically, the psychologist James Lynch found that children who experience early failure in learning to read at school are more likely to develop high blood pressure early in life and to have shortened life spans.[18] Early elementary-school learning, which has such enormous consequences for children's future, depends on children being able to receive instruction from authority figures. That ability is less likely to develop smoothly in children of socially isolated parents. Once again, the problem of social isolation has unlikely and extremely far-reaching consequences.

Reliance on Substances Instead of People

For many, the problem of feeling isolated and left out has an easy solution: have a drink or a pill that makes you feel better. There is no need to call anyone up or make it clear that you're lonely. It is a do-it-yourself solution that has worked for humans since history began. Sometimes socializing is a by-product of substance use (as it was reliably in the television tavern of *Cheers*). Sometimes, socializing follows as an explicit therapeutic benefit of substance use (as it does in the successful treatment of depression with anti-depressant medication). Sometimes, the treatment of substance abuse is itself a better cure for social isolation than anything available to people *without* substance-abuse problems (as is the case with Alcoholics Anonymous, probably the most reliable antidote to loneliness ever invented in this country). But before a hand reaches for a drink or a pill, there is often a feeling of aloneness.

When citizens of a nation of independent individuals start depending on drugs and alcohol as a preferred alternative to depending on people, some problems are solved and new problems are created. One problem that we see often in our own practices is lonely, scared individuals wondering who they really are. When taking mood-modifying medications, even those prescribed by thoughtful, sensitive psychiatrists, many patients find their relief is tempered by worries that they do not know how they *really* feel. There are anxious asides and uneasy jokes along the lines of "I don't know what is the drug and what is me." Psychiatrists are skillful at offering reassuring responses to those worries, but the questions remain philosophically daunting. So patients end up feeling better but often remain mistrustful of their improvements. And while the difference may be clear at the extremes, where to draw the line between ordinary unhappiness, which is best treated with ordinary human caring, and disease states, which are best treated by medical intervention, remains confusing. It is not yet clear when an individual needs medication to help him rejoin the surrounding community and when he just needs to be held by that community in its healing bonds.

Then there are the drugs of abuse, most of them illegal but at least one of them (alcohol) not only legal but with a time-honored role in social gatherings and human connection. Each substance has its crowd of loyal followers who swear that it allows entry into experiences of creativity and sensual pleasure that cannot be reached in any other way. If you take the drug, you can join the club. Drug use in fact can supply an automatic network of companions who socialize together because they all share an interest and an activity (the drug use). Some substances, like alcohol, even make it easier for shy and lonely strangers to enjoy one another's company. A sociologist writing about alcohol in the 1940s described its purpose with the wonderfully apt phrase "social jollification."[19] We frequently hear socially awkward college students say that they have to use alcohol or drugs because it's the only way they know to be part of a group. They are very clear that they are using drugs to cure loneliness, but, as they poignantly explain, they can't find any other way. Sometimes, at least, the cure is successful and drug use does allow entry into a network of friends. For the lucky ones, the friendships may even begin to extend into life beyond drug use. But all too often, the drug itself becomes the friend. A patient who descended into two years of alcohol abuse after the end of her marriage was very clear about it. She called her bottle of red wine "my best friend." Looking back on those two years from the vantage point of her first month of sobriety, she added, "I understand why I called it my best friend. In the afternoon, I feel so completely alone. That's what I didn't have to feel when I was drinking. I'm fortunate. I don't seem to have whatever it is in some people's genes that makes them compulsive drinkers. But I can't stand feeling alone like that, wanting [my husband] to come back. I don't know what to do when I get home in the afternoon and I can't open a bottle of wine."

As our patient suggests, substance abuse is a complex phenomenon. It almost certainly does not have a single cause. But the substance abuse of a great many individuals is fueled by their experiences of social rejection and social isolation. The rising rate of depression and the rising numbers of both adults and children who use antidepressant medication is also fueled (again, in part) by their experiences of social rejection and social isolation. These changes have occurred in the context of major social changes in the United States—as networks of confidants have fallen away, as the number of individuals living alone has skyrocketed, as social capital has declined. A study of 389 American cities found that deaths from alcoholism and suicide increase when people live alone.[20] It would be foolish to ignore these correlations, even as we recognize that the use of psychoactive substances (whether for recreation or for treatment) is a complex phenomenon that has more than one cause.

Shedding Obligations While Courting Depression

The ideal for many people who grew up during the course of the last fifty years has been a life free from the social obligations that seemed to drive their parents (or at least their mothers) into chronic irritable moods, with quiet mutterings about "too much to do." Those mothers often felt overburdened by all the caretaking that was their responsibility and all the social connections that they were expected to maintain—with their extended families, with their friends, with the people who mattered to their husbands' careers, with their neighbors, and with even larger communities—all without getting the kind of general acknowledgment of social importance that was granted to their husbands' careers. It should be no surprise that their daughters and sons (and now their granddaughters and grandsons) want to be free of the stress that comes from too much caretaking, too many social obligations, too much *connection*. But we have overshot and created a new array of discontents.

If a life freed from social obligations is a better life, why are people not happier? Happiness and well-being in the United States have been declining in studies conducted over the last twenty-five years.[21] If a life freed from social obligations is a better life, why are people more likely to be depressed? Rates of depression in this country have been rising steadily in studies conducted over the last fifty years.[22] Alexis de Tocqueville observed that "Americans of all ages, all conditions and all dispositions constantly form associations."[23] We are no longer a nation of associations, either formal or informal. In the realm of informal social connections, the major changes are the result of a shift in women's roles away from caretaking and connection, with little sign that men are picking up the slack. The shift in women's roles is partly a straightforward response to their new obligations in the workplace. A woman can only do so much. But the relative neglect of associations is a choice made by both men and women who saw their mothers' worn looks and decided to shy away from responsibility for social connectedness.

In our advice to the lonely, we often emphasize a time-honored approach: try to engineer into your life regular contact and shared projects with potentially interesting people. It's the old "join a church choir" strategy. Shared commitments, shared *obligations*, continue to be the most reliable paths to friendship and sometimes more. In earlier times, however, there was no need to engineer social obligation into one's life. It was there waiting, uninvited. People *had* to take care of one another, and social connections followed. Whether it was the burial societies of new immigrant groups who wished to avoid paupers' graves or the quilting bees of women who merged necessary labor with socializing, a reliable social fabric was very hard to avoid. If an aging parent was ailing, the grown child took that parent into his or her own home because there was no other choice. If sons or daughters remained unmarried, they lived with their parents because (usually) anything else was unaffordable. Divorce was mostly avoided because the economic cost and social stigma were both too much to bear. If someone in the neighborhood or parish was homebound, people mobilized for meal preparation and delivery out of simple duty, whether civic or religious.

In our practices, we see patients who are so fed up with the difficulty of dealing with aging parents or siblings that they look to us for an expert's pronouncement that they must end all contact. We see parents of adult children who look for the same liberating advice about cutting off their children. Our professional dispensation is sought so that our patients may turn away from family obligations with clear consciences. It must be done for the sake of their mental health. Our own experience watching these dramas over the years has led us to believe that cutting these ties ends up hurting the one who cuts as much as it hurts the one who is cut. In the end, both feel cut off and adrift. It is rarely the simple surgical excision that our patients hope for. Most of them gradually become depressed in their newfound freedom. We have gradually come to the conclusion that, in the absence of egregious abuse, a person is better off struggling to improve a bad relationship with a close relative, or simply finding ways to tolerate it, than severing the tie completely.

We think that obligations have gotten a bad rap. People who feel that they should only see others when they really feel like it will, over time, tend to see less and less of people. It is another example of the paradox of choice. If you spend much time ruminating over whether you *really* feel like seeing someone while also wondering if there is something else you would rather do, you quickly lose the rhythm of regular connection that keeps people feeling close to one another. A sense of obligation turns out to be the glue that holds people together during rough patches. That glue is essential, because there are always rough patches, in any relationship.

A web of relationships is like a hammock that holds a person safely above the hard ground of depression; a web of relationships is also like a snare that holds a person back from the freshness of new possibilities. It's never easy to get the balance right, but when a person sheds too many obligations because they feel more like a snare than a hammock, he may shed the very connections that keep him from going to ground.

CHAPTER 9

Social Disconnection and the Mental Health Industry

When people live alone or lose touch with confidants, they lose the reflections of themselves in others' eyes that helps them know who they are and what they are like. A job may offer some perspective, but roles in the workplace are only a part of who people are. What we learn about ourselves from bosses and coworkers is different from what we learn from close friends, familiar relatives, and housemates. One place that socially isolated individuals turn to gain perspective on themselves and their lives is television. A woman recently sent us a copy of a letter she had written to Dr. Phil. His show on "bully husbands" had helped her to look at her own life. Others may turn to psychology books or Internet chat sites. Still others will consult mental health professionals, usually after long periods of solitary worry. The particular twists and turns that the worrying takes may vary, shaped by each person's life story, but at the heart of it is a simple fear: "Is there something wrong with me?" That fear builds in solitude, and the individual finally ends up in a professional's office.

Once he or she is there, the fear will almost certainly be approached from the perspective of individual pathology, preferably with a clear diagnostic label, despite all the evidence that increasing social isolation is a societal problem. Both patient and clinician have a vested interest in the discovery of a diagnosis. For the clinician, a diagnosis makes clear that specialized expertise has led to a precise understanding of the problem, and specialized expertise is necessary to treat it—the specialized expertise that is the source of the clinician's livelihood. For the patient, a diagnosis provides an explanation for loneliness and unhappiness, which is itself a powerful source of relief even when nothing else has changed. But of course, everything changes with a diagnosis, including the patient's social world. A diagnosis now offers a lonely individual more hope for reconnecting with other people than almost any other route. A diagnosis gives one a psychotherapist and perhaps a psychopharmacologist too. It connects the person with a group of people who share the same diagnosis. It invites the patient to join those people and participate with them in meetings to overcome their shared problems or to spread knowledge about their shared condition. It even makes it easier to reconnect with lost friends and relatives because it gives a blame-free explanation for past difficulties. The problems weren't the individual's fault. The problems weren't the fault of friends or family. The problems were the illness's fault. A diagnosis helps in so many ways that have nothing to do with a specific treatment of a specific illness. A diagnosis also conveniently opens the door to insurance reimbursement for the help that is received. The only downside to a diagnosis is that it completely shifts attention away from the surrounding social forces that have also created the problems. And (as we shall see) it provides patients with relationships that, while unquestionably helpful, turn out to be bad models for relationships with anyone but paid helpers.

Some Psychiatric Syndromes of Our Time

First, let us look at some diagnoses that are all tangled up with social isolation, cocooning, and what we have called being "frantic without a peep." Depression and anxiety, the most common diagnoses, are certainly interwoven with these issues, but the connections are in many ways obvious (though not uncomplicated—for example, when does depression cause loneliness and when does loneliness cause depression?). We will focus instead on several syndromes that illustrate how a psychiatric diagnosis can patch together a frayed network of social support. Anorexia, bulimia, self-mutilation, and alcohol abuse, particularly in adolescent girls and young women, are good examples. Since one of the authors is a child psychiatrist and a woman, we see and hear about these patients frequently. The conditions themselves are more common now than they were a half a century ago. Most often, the patient is a girl who has tried very hard not to be an additional burden for an overstressed parent (or parents) who already seems to be barely holding her head above water. In the process of growing up, these young women try to devise strategies to manage their own burdens of anxiety and competition, at school and among their peers, without complaining to parents. Sometimes these strategies started out as healthy habits—like exercise and attention to diet, or a mix of determined self-discipline and an occasional drink with friends to unwind—but get out of control and take on lives of their own, morphing into symptoms like binge eating, binge drinking, cutting, and starvation. These symptoms all have an added benefit. Not only do they provide ways to manage anxiety and other intolerable feeling states, they also function as signals, a way to communicate distress without complaining. The message to their parents is *I too am barely holding my head above water. Even though I never complain, you need to notice that I am not really managing things.* These symptoms, even when they are desperately hidden, cry out for attention and start to tighten an overstretched bond with parents—and sometimes with friends or teachers.

Many of these young women do have friends. Their loneliness is not all-pervasive. They might not tell their parents much, but they do communicate with other teenagers. Psychiatrists cannot help but notice how often groups of friends will acquire these syndromes together. Shared symptoms, like shared diagnoses, can be a powerful bond, bringing friends even closer. This is why psychological symptoms can be contagious (or even competitive). A recent study found that teenage girls develop more severe symptoms if they talk together too much about their problems.[1] The same symptoms that demand attention from an overwhelmed parent also shore up bonds with friends. Again, with an added benefit—all this social support is mobilized without the teenager uttering a peep. Self-reliance has run amok. These girls have found the perfect solution for families that have lost the habit of constructive complaint and the skills of asking directly for help or advice or affection from one another. Instead, the self-destructive symptom serves to mobilize support. But the support function usually ends up being handed off to professionals by terrified parents who (appropriately) don't trust their own responses to such dangerous behavior. Once the handoff is made, the support gets bundled with formal diagnoses, extensive treatment plans, and a whole new set of relationships within the mental health system. Soon these diagnoses become part of a family's identity, drawing family members a little closer to one another and often to other families with similar problems. The diagnosis becomes an essential tool in the reconstruction of social connection, even as it is a source of sadness with no particular endpoint.

We cannot say too often that most psychiatric illnesses are caused by a complicated interplay of underlying biology, life events, and social circumstances. It is not all about social support. It is, however, almost always *also* about social support. That is clearly true for substance abuse and alcoholism, even when we expand our view beyond teenage girls. These so-called illnesses (a hundred-year-old debate over the appropriateness of the medical model continues to this day[2]) have everything to do with connection and disconnection. Just as some people have described alcohol as a social lubricant that helps calm social anxiety, drinking alone has long been seen as a worrisome sign of impending alcoholism. Substance abuse is often a substitute for depending on other people. We will not repeat that argument, which we already presented in the previous chapter. We just want to highlight another way that a diagnosis can serve as a powerful tool for rebuilding fragmented social networks. With these addictions defined as illnesses, a whole rehabilitation industry now works to connect an addict with others who are fighting to get over their own addictions, building powerful bonds of shared struggle and shared aspirations that can transform sobriety from an inconceivable goal into a possible one. These treatments harness the power of not having to face a challenge alone. That power is available if one will simply say the words "I am an alcoholic" (or "an addict"). Organizations such as Alcoholics Anonymous and its offshoots allow an immediate escape from loneliness, an instant support network that enfolds the participant no matter what town he or she may be in, alone or afraid. AA also currently provides the strongest support for the disease concept of alcoholism.[3] The bond starts with a diagnosis. It provides an identity and a peer group. It allows someone to start over, to reinvent a life. Symptom as signal, diagnosis as identity, and treatment as social network; the sequence is now a common solution to the problem of loneliness in America. A diagnosis provides the social network of last resort.

There are also psychiatric syndromes in which patients lose the thread of who they are or how they look. One such syndrome is body dysmorphic disorder (BDD). Patients with BDD suffer intensely. They look in the mirror and think that they are hideous beyond belief. They feel they must hide themselves away until they can remedy the problems, or, if they fear the problems are unfixable, they set about changing their lives so they will never have to be seen. The character of the Phantom of the Opera probably gives some sense of what it is like to have BDD, except that beneath the mask in BDD there is a perfectly normal and some-times very attractive face. Usually patients have discovered some tiny defects and blown them completely out of proportion. In their haste to hide themselves in shame, they lose the opportunity to experience others gazing at them without horror, an experience that can help them return to their senses. A mainstay of treatment (along with SSRI medications) is a type of therapy called exposure with response prevention.[4] In BDD, this approach often involves requiring patients to enter social situations without making the usual moves to hide the imagined defects. It is an agonizing effort, but gradually the patient is able to comprehend that the expected looks of horror and rejection never appear. In other words, treat-ment involves an intense counter-pressure against the pull of so-cial isolation. Once again, the etiology of BDD is complex and not fully understood, but a drift into more severe symptoms is likely to last longer and progress further in a society that allows most drifts into social isolation to go unnoticed or even to be seen as ordinary. We all need the perspective of others to know who we are. Once we start to distort that perspective in our own minds, unchecked by real-world encounters, terrible things can happen. A general trend toward social fragmentation increases the risk.

A Curious Connection

A diagnosis, or simply a decision to consult a mental health pro-fessional, brings a new brand of connection into a person's life. When a person seeks help from a psychotherapist, he or she might encounter someone like one of us. We get excited when we meet new patients and start to feel that we can be helpful to them. The patients also might feel a bit excited by the idea that we can help them "get better." Soon, patient and therapist are deeply involved in an interesting and unusual relationship that is governed by a curious set of rules. The rules are quite different from the rules for ordinary relationships. The most striking difference is that the usual expectation of reciprocity disappears. Patients get to talk mostly about themselves. Patients are *expected* to talk mostly about themselves. There is (at least in theory) no need to worry about the therapist's state of mind, or whether the therapist might rather be talking about something else, perhaps even him- or herself. The job of the therapist is to be curious about the patient. When a patient is curious about a therapist, the therapist's job is to use that curiosity to illuminate the *patient's* mind, not to kick back and talk about the hard day at the office or what problems are waiting at home. The mental health professional has spent years of training with a single goal—to provide patients with reliable attention and understanding, keeping the focus on the patient's problems and life and words. There is no expectation of equal time. On the contrary, there is a professional duty to refuse any offers of equal time. If a patient is in a bad mood, any concern for the other person in the room can simply be dropped. And there is a similarly one-sided rule about confidentiality—therapists guarantee their patients' confidentiality, but patients can say whatever they want about their therapists to anyone they please.

These rules have helped to create a very effective treatment. The claim that psychotherapy (or, more accurately, a range of psychotherapies) leads to significant relief of suffering and improvement in the lives of patients is now backed by a vast body of careful research.[5] But it can lead some patients down the garden path. It looks much like those confiding relationships that the General Social Survey has been tracking, relationships with relatives, friends, spouses, and coworkers. But it is a bad model for any of those relationships, at least if people want them to last, because most confidants eventually want equal time. The special partnership that allows a therapist to earn a good living and a patient to focus on neglected aspects of his life and experience would be a disaster outside of the office. Used as a template for other intimate relationships, it is selfish and self-absorbed. Other than therapists, only an occasional very self-sacrificing parent or a spouse who aspires to martyrdom is likely to sign on for that long-term. A problem with psychotherapy is that it can make all other relationships look like they fall short when it comes to sustained, attentive caring and leave the patient circling back to therapy as the only relationship that is good enough.

Therapists have their own version of the same problem. Real-world relationships can sometimes pale beside the intensity of time spent with patients who ask that you fight valiantly alongside them to transform their lives. And there is reason to suspect that people who become skilled at observing others likely felt a little left out themselves when they were young. Standing on the sidelines (looking for a way in) is a good place to acquire the skills of a psychologically astute observer. Once that feeling is part of a person's identity, a special relationship in which one is essential to a patient's well-being, and maybe even a patient's very survival, is almost redemptive. So therapists who need to be needed are less likely to worry about the other real and potential relationships that treatment might be supplanting—for both the patient and the therapist. While in theory, all therapists subscribe to the idea of tying patients back in to a rich social network (or helping them create a network of relationships for the first time), they may be reluctant to encourage and reinforce real-life relationships when both their livelihoods and their self-esteem might suffer. Just as parents may have trouble encouraging their teenagers to build the relationships with peers that will start to loosen the wonderfully gratifying ties between parent and child that once flourished, therapists often spend more energy analyzing the patient-therapist relationship than using what they learn to encourage the repair of old relationships and the construction of new ones. There is no question that psychotherapy can remove barriers that keep patients from forming satisfying relationships. But psychotherapy also has the potential to disrupt or block other relationships. Too little attention has been paid to this danger, both in practice and in research.[6] As the ordinary difficulties of maintaining social connections increase, more attention must be paid to an important potential side effect of otherwise helpful psychotherapy.

However, our concern about self-absorption in psychotherapy may become less important, not because of changes within psychotherapy but because of changes around it. In an earlier chapter, we mentioned a study that found a 30 percent increase in narcissism among college students over a twenty-five-year period. More college students happen to be in mental health treatment than ever before, but they have no need to turn to psychotherapy as the sole available outlet for self-absorption. New technologies have created so many more interesting possibilities for those who want to maintain the focus on themselves as fascinating entities, like blogging, MySpace, YouTube, and whatever is about to come next. Older patients still occasionally express an uneasiness to us —they worry that psychotherapy is too self-indulgent, too self-absorbed. That worry may soon disappear. There are now so many interesting alternatives to reciprocal relationships.

How Psychotherapy Helps the Lonely

Nevertheless, a good therapist can help a lonely person in many ways, some obvious and some more obscure. First, there is the relief of getting back into communication with another human being about "matters of importance." Essentially, the first benefit of psychotherapy is that it offers a confiding relationship to an individual who may lack other confidants. A patient may initially complain, "How will talking about my problems help anyway?," but everyone knows (or quickly discovers) that there is real relief in finding someone who listens sympathetically to worries that have been echoing around in one's mind for weeks or months or years. What psychotherapy also offers (something that is not a reliable part of the deal with friends or relatives) is the freedom to share strong emotions without cleaning them up first. Soon the lonely patient is not feeling quite so alone or quite so different from the rest of the human race.

Most therapists hope that this relief will have an automatic ripple effect as patients remember the pleasure and ease that communication about important matters affords. The hope is that it will jump-start the patients' other relationships, whether by reconnecting with people from whom patients have stepped away or by making new connections. If that next step does not follow, most therapists will try to understand what baggage from the past—life experience or patterns of thought or lack of social skills—might be getting in the way. The particular focus and preferred solutions may vary somewhat based on the therapist's training, but the end result is likely to be similar: the patient's new or reawakened ability to connect with others both casually and intimately. Therapy at its best permits people to reestablish active social networks in their lives.

The combination of a confiding relationship, the exploration of particular barriers to relationships, and the attention to changing the habits of thought and behavior that strained relationships in the past can be enormously effective in bringing a lonely person back into circulation. But even when all the work is done and a patient is poised and seemingly ready to reenter circulation, nothing may happen. Part of the problem may lie in the seductive self-absorption of psychotherapy already discussed. Part of the problem may also be simple rustiness. When people avoid real-life intimate relationships for a period of time, they start to feel anxious about stepping back in. They are out of practice, no matter how well-rehearsed they feel in therapy. Patients sometimes assume that if therapy was working well, they would not feel any anxiety about getting back into the world of nontherapy relationships. They forget about the "rustiness phenomenon," which means that whenever someone tries to reenter relationships after avoiding them for a while, anxiety will be a part of the experience. Patients who are waiting for therapy to make all their anxiety vanish will wait forever.

Therapy can also create greater distance in a patient's other intimate relations, if the patient is not completely isolated to start with. Once again, it is not just that therapy provides a problematic template for intimacy; it is that it offers its own compelling intimacy that can make other confidants seem superfluous. After all, the therapist is so much better at listening than "amateurs." A spouse may feel pangs of jealousy when he or she realizes that the partner is sharing all the really juicy tidbits of their life with a therapist or has shifted discussions of really important matters out of the marriage and into the therapy. What patient wants to waste a relationship that is so special and expensive? Why not bring in everything of importance for scrutiny? Gradually, the patient's real-life relationships can begin to feel pallid. The heart has been taken out of them, and they lose their value. And since we are talking about lonely people, most of these patients begin therapy feeling somewhat estranged from spouses and friends, so the system is fragile to start with. When a patient reaches the point of being ready to end estrangement from others but still seems paralyzed, it may be because the individual faces a bigger step than he or she would have had to take before the treatment began.

Our awareness of these dangers has led us to make some adjustments in our own approaches. First, we encourage patients to share with their partners (if they have them) much of what comes up in therapy. We want to make sure that the partner doesn't feel chronically left out because of the treatment. Second, we try to stay very alert to a patient's existing relationships, taking seriously the Hippocratic maxim, "First, do no harm," and hopefully even strengthening those relationships. Third, we allow enough of our real (that is, nonprofessional) selves to be visible to our patients so that we do not become mysteriously fascinating gurus whose pronouncements have a value that cannot be matched by the insights of spouses, friends, and family. We even offer opinions, intentionally sacrificing the aura of omniscience that depends on never taking a position that can be proved wrong. Fourth, we emphasize the important role of loneliness and feeling left out in *everyone's* life. We help the patient to realize that there is nothing unique or especially pathetic about an ordinary life experience. We might even use ourselves as examples so we are not talking from on high about the sad plight of those poor people who lack our extensive knowledge. Finally, we do not hesitate to bring a patient's family members into the therapy when we think it would be helpful. We believe it is just as important to protect a patient's other relationships from the possibly damaging effects of therapy as it is to protect the therapy from the possibly damaging intrusions of family members.

One effect of these changes is that we seem quite real to our patients. Having our offices in our home (with occasional interruptions by UPS deliveries and plumbers) adds to the sense that we have no special magic. In some ways, that is a loss. Magical doctors can achieve magical cures. But what our patients get in return is a sense that their struggles with loneliness and rejection make them human rather than peculiar. It opens up the possibility of ordinary solutions to the ordinary problems of social isolation, even when they must be supplemented by an understanding of a specific patient's particular obstacles. It offers a sense of connection with others that does not begin with a diagnosis.

The Promise of Magical Medicines

Turn on the television most nights and you will learn that there is no reason to put up with pain or allergies or insomnia or bad moods any longer. Just ask your doctor for a prescription, and the problem will disappear. Who hasn't watched those commercials and longed for the pretty green luna moth of Lunesta fame to bring on deep childlike sleep with lovely dreams instead of the sometimes interrupted sleep of a worried adult? People have come to our offices in search of prescriptions for stimulants, not because they had attention deficit disorder, but because they were hoping to improve their (or their children's) SAT scores. We see patients who want those same stimulants for weight loss or want antidepressants to make them into less irritable parents. We see parents who want a medication that will change the character of a willful child. There are many studies that show psychotherapy is as effective as medication for a wide range of psychiatric difficulties, but why not just take a pill instead? In fact, almost everyone can think of some burdensome problem that can now be improved with psychoactive medicines. If the particular primary care physician or psychiatrist or pediatrician who is consulted first balks, most people simply look for a more cooperative doctor. What is a psychiatrist who's trying to hold tight to her integrity to do?

Years ago, one of the authors wrote about how emerging psychiatric medications might lead the medical field to look at inborn characteristics in a whole new way.[7] That certainly has turned out to be true. Shyness is a good example. With evidence that SSRIs can reduce social anxiety, the boundary between shyness (which is a matter of temperament) and social anxiety (which is a formal psychiatric disorder) is shifting. What was once seen as part of the normal spectrum gets redefined as an illness requiring treatment. Shyness is an inborn trait. While it is reasonably stable over time, it is also often overcome by children as they grow up. With a medication available to reduce social anxiety, will we as a society become less tolerant of shyness? Will we demand that it be treated? And will that be a good thing for society as a whole? Or might there be some advantages in having people with a range of characteristics that are occasionally annoying, occasionally burdensome, but frequently useful? A society of extroverts may not be an entirely desirable goal. If social reticence becomes an illness that requires treatment, the pathologizing of loneliness will soar off the charts. We also worry that the enthusiasm with which parents search for medications that will make children get better grades and be more obedient may go hand in hand with a neglect of the hard work of parenting that's necessary to encourage the growth of true curiosity and the ability to take instruction.

We understand that as long as medications promise to bring happiness in life and success in school and career, people will to be tempted. We also know that as doctors, we have a job to relieve suffering and to improve the quality of our patients' lives, not to quibble with them about how to get there. Our prescription pads are not locked away in some hard-to-reach drawer. We have seen lives saved and lives transformed by psychiatric medications. But we have also seen systematic neglect of potentially serious side effects of medications and systematic neglect of alternatives to medication that seem less magical because they look so much like ordinary life—and lack the deep pockets of an immensely profitable industry to fund extensive research that fills the scientific journals and extensive advertising that floods the airwaves. A good example is light therapy, which (like psychotherapy) provides a potent alternative to medication in the treatment of depression, with fewer side effects.[8] Social support and human connection are a little like sunlight: they are so ordinary that their miraculous powers barely get any attention.

The Mental Health Point of View

A mental health point of view can be corrosive to one's sense of self. In an oversimplified way, it seems to say, *If you are not feeling good, you must be suffering from some kind of pathology. Just go to your local mental health professional, who will offer a diagnosis and then tweak you chemically and psychologically until you feel right again.* But there are many obstacles to feeling good beyond people's own pathologies. When the brain is functioning well, it has a wide array of alarm systems that alerts the individual to danger. If those alarm systems are healthy, people are not always happy. A crucial alarm system is exquisitely sensitive to social exclusion and social isolation. When that alarm is sounding, a person feels distress. The distress *is* the alarm. Its purpose is to get the person to do something about the danger. Ignoring or quieting the distress without solving the problems of social exclusion or isolation is a risky strategy. It is risky because social isolation is stressful, whether people feel the distress or not. It leads to poorer functioning, poorer health, and shorter lives. It leads to pathology in the human organism. But the underlying pathology is increasingly located in our society rather than in the individual. So people should not expect to feel good all the time, and when they are not feeling good, it might be best to start trying to feel better by reconnecting with friends and relatives, checking in, comparing notes, and regaining some perspective on the worries of the moment, before they head off to the local mental health professionals for diagnosis and treatment.

It is true that if everyone followed our advice, we'd be out of a job (or at least we would have a narrower job to do—there would still be psychiatric illnesses in need of treatment). And we would be sadder for it, since our work has been very gratifying over the last thirty years. But when we consider the far-reaching consequences of each lonely person pursuing a relationship with a psychotherapist or a psychopharmacologist as the standard response to problems of loneliness and social isolation, we see a widening problem rather than a solution. A torn social fabric in which people have no confidence in their friends and family and neighbors as a source of help or solace is too high a price to pay for a wide scope of psychiatric practice.

CHAPTER 10

Staying Limber

Let us try to strip our ideas down to their most essential elements. Then we will risk stretching our argument a little too far with some ideas about what should be done.

We began with a simple but compelling fact from the General Social Survey: in the past twenty years, the number of Americans who have talked to *no one* about something of importance to them during the previous six months has skyrocketed. That number is now a quarter of the population. In all the debates about how socially connected we are to one another as a nation, that fact stands out. Whatever the average connectedness might be (and there is convincing evidence that average connectedness has also declined), a socially isolated core has now grown too large to be ignored.

We then explored the cultural and psychological factors that currently shape so many small but life-altering choices that push people in the direction of greater disconnection. We described both a push and a pull. The push is the increasing franticness of daily life, which makes one want to step back whenever possible to reduce the deafening background noise. The pull is the American ideal of the self-reliant loner-hero, which can make stepping back feel like a badge of superiority.

Next, we examined the effects that stepping back has on an individual. We found that the experience of social exclusion, seemingly so petty, is in fact so powerful, so deeply embedded in both
neurobiology and personal experience, that it takes hold and starts
to reshape a person's feelings, thinking, and behavior—even when
the individual has unknowingly left him- or herself out by small
steps back. We also found that once people have left themselves
out, it is very hard to find a way back in, partly because a set of
slightly paranoid feelings take over and people stop trying.

Finally, we looked at the consequences of social disconnection,
which turn out to be both extensive and remarkably diverse. Social isolation reduces happiness, health, and longevity. It increases
aggression. It increases substance abuse. It correlates with increasing rates of violent crime. It probably reduces the effectiveness of democratic government. And it squanders the world's
resources in environmentally damaging ways.

So what next?

Awareness

As clinicians, we know that much of our work with patients assumes that awareness makes a difference. Moving a problem into
the foreground, or even better, moving a patient's unwitting contribution to the problem into the foreground, often opens up a
range of new possibilities and responses that were previously inconceivable. As clinicians, we also regularly rediscover that awareness does not always do the trick. It is, however, a place to start.

It is incredibly difficult to resist or even to detect cultural
forces and see how they affect people's actions in everyday life. We
wrote this book in order to bring our country's hidden cultural values and unwitting choices out of the closet, so people won't som-
nambulate their way to lonely despair without even recognizing
how or why they are doing it. The truth is that if one can bring
oneself to acknowledge loneliness, half the battle is won. It is not

an easy half of a battle, however. When we began to talk about these ideas with friends, their usual first response was to passionately defend their own styles of staying disconnected. Having chosen, like so many Americans, to step back, they explain how right the choice has been for them. It is exactly that kind of reflexive claim—we chose it, so it must make us happy—that traps people. The argument that people are happier when they can spend more time alone seems to make so much sense on a daily basis, yet over the course of a life (and a country's life) it is simply wrong. A problem cannot be solved when people refuse to call it by its rightful name. And a problem cannot be solved by saying that it is already solved, by people publicly insisting that they are happier alone. The medical evidence tells us otherwise. The happiness research tells us otherwise. Statistics on crime and substance abuse tell us otherwise. Yes, we all need balance in our lives. We all need time away from the crowd. But we also need one another—and feeling left out, *even when one has chosen to be left out*, is not satisfying. It is painful!

An analogy with the country's battle against obesity is helpful. The outcome is not determined by any single or even several decisive moments. The outcome for each individual is determined by the almost numberless small choices he or she makes, day after day. To succeed, one must often make choices that, in the moment, increases rather than decreases anxiety. (And even the success of the battle against obesity is affected by feeling left out. Remember the research that showed individuals eating more cookies, choosing unhealthy snacks, and lying around more after being socially excluded.)

We find further parallels in studies of television watching. Watching TV for a small amount of time relaxes us. Watching TV for a long amount of time depresses us. And isolates us. The social effects of television also shed light on today's hopes that a technological "fix" for isolation has been created with the Internet and cell phones. A startling article appeared in *Woman's Day* in the early 1950s that celebrated the coming of television as a boon to family life, bringing family members back together from the solitude of their own rooms and their own radios. The effects of a new technology is not intrinsic to the technology itself. It will be determined by the small, everyday choices people will make about how they use technology. Those choices will in turn be shaped automatically and unconsciously by our country's dominant cultural myths—unless we can make ourselves aware of them and choose more knowingly.

Small daily choices end up defining one's social world—whether to go to a local store or order off the Internet; whether to pick up a ringing telephone or let it go to voice mail; whether to get together with a friend for coffee or pop a DVD into the home theater. These little decisions are powerful because they are cumulative and because they fuel a vicious cycle. You step back a little from others. They step back a little from you. You feel a little left out. Feeling left out, when that feeling is unexamined, leads you to step back farther. Feeling left out, when examined, can lead you to work a little harder to reconnect.

Sometimes it really does take work. One of the cheerful memories we have of our New England winters is the warmth and conviviality of our street after a snowstorm, shovel-wielding neighbors exhausted but glad to see one another emerging into a shared experience. And glad to take a break, leaning on our shovels, to talk about "important matters." A few years ago, one of the authors looked up from shoveling to discover that all the other shovels on the street were wielded not by neighbors, but by hired crews. Something small but important to the neighborhood had been lost. The example is trivial, but that is exactly the point. So many of the choices people make about whether to put themselves in situations that lead naturally to connections with others are trivial. Each one matters very little. It is easy to fool oneself into believing that the next choice will balance it out. But the dynamics of feeling left out makes that less and less likely, and the evidence is that the balance has shifted. The example of our street after a snowstorm also makes clear that what has changed is the nation's culture, not individual abilities: the neighbors who were still out on the street with shovels were the older ones.

An awareness of the risks of social disconnection can also change the bigger decisions that people make—like whether to work from home whenever possible or to work alongside others; whether to live alone whenever possible or to live with others. People regularly make those choices based on what they think they are supposed to want, even when their own experiences tell them it is a mistake.

Jenny is a bright young woman who just graduated from an Ivy League college. She plans to move from Boston to New York City to start her first job. During college, she was often lonely. She had a single room through most of her college years. It was her choice. "I like having my own space," she said, even though she was always wishing that there was a more interesting social life going on in her space. Now, she explained to Jacqueline, her therapist, it had always been her dream to have an apartment of her own in New York City. When Jacqueline wondered whether living alone was a good idea in light of her loneliness, which she'd experienced even when she'd played team sports and was surrounded by people her own age in college, the patient was surprised. The power of a romantic cultural myth—a young woman alone in the big city— was so great that it had never occurred to Jenny to question it. Most of the time, when personal experience contradicts a cultural myth, what gets dismissed is the personal experience. That is, unless there is the chance to compare notes with others who are questioning the same myth.

Education

Closely related to awareness is education, which amounts to an opportunity to compare notes with others who are questioning the same myth. The effects of social connection on health and longevity, well documented by several decades of medical research, is beginning to be more widely acknowledged. A recent spate of books about positive psychology and happiness research is spreading the same message about social connection and happiness. Public health education regularly tries to make individuals aware of unseen consequences of seemingly trivial daily choices. The effects of health education are usually mixed, but there are certainly fewer smokers and more people exercising today than there would have been if the consequences of those choices had not been spelled out over and over again, so often that they entered the category of general knowledge.

Becoming educated about the health effects of social isolation can tip the balance in the internal debate that the average person has at the end of a too-busy workday about whether to collapse into quiet solitude or to call a friend. Abstract arguments about social fabric will never provide the push that enlightened self-interest offers in those marginal moments of our lives. Similarly, becoming educated about the vicious cycle of stepping back, feeling left out, and finally becoming set in one's own lonely ways can provide a reason to stay limber and be responsive to the social possibilities of the moment rather than dismissing them with a why-bother shrug.

Using awareness and education to open up the possibility of a fresh response to an old problem is basic to all psychotherapies. Once a patient becomes aware of a problem and arrives at an understanding that includes his or her own (previously unnoticed) contributions to the problem (psychoanalysts use the word *unconscious*, cognitive therapists prefer the word *automatic*), all sorts of new ideas emerge. A patient can begin to try and do things differently. Even with awareness and understanding, trying to do things differently generates a lot of anxiety and often goes badly at first, but gradually people get the hang of it. If the result is a more successful or satisfying life, then a vicious cycle gets replaced with a virtuous one.

In a talk he gave toward the end of his life, the famous behaviorist B. F. Skinner said that behavior therapists had come to rely too much on artificial reinforcements within the treatment. The most effective way to change behavior, he believed, was to harness the natural reinforcements in a person's environment. The pleasures of being held in the embrace of family and friends is certainly one of those natural reinforcements. On the other hand, so are the pleasures of peace and quiet and solitude. Life is all about balance. If, as we suggest, the balance has tipped too far in the direction of disconnection, perhaps there are natural correctives already in play. And if there are, supporting those natural correctives is likely to be a much more effective strategy than any polemic about the benefits of social engagement.

Natural Correctives

When Robert Putnam put forth his ideas in *Bowling Alone* about the decline of social capital, several sociologists argued that even if some old associations (like bowling leagues) had declined, new associations (like soccer leagues) were sprouting up as they always had. From their point of view, there was no cause for alarm. The pendulum is always swinging back and forth. People know how to make corrections when some cultural trend starts pushing their lives out of balance. Obviously, we believe there really is cause for alarm. As we mentioned, the sociologists who discovered the dramatic drop in confidants began their study expecting to prove Putnam wrong and ended up supporting his ideas. And stepping back does trigger a process that traps many people and leads them to give up on corrective action. However, there are some hopeful signs.

A recent article in the *New York Times* caught our attention. It was about life in the rarefied world of Manhattan condominiums, a world of high incomes, high ambitions, and an abundance of people living alone (remember that 48 percent of all households in Manhattan are single-person households). The article, titled "A Beautiful Day in the Neighborhood,"[1] describes a new condominium building in which residents can enjoy free breakfast in a common space that's meant to foster relationships among condo owners. Other condo developments around the city are organizing weekly get-togethers so that inhabitants of what could so easily be a lonely and disconnected dwelling can make friends in their building-village. Real estate professionals in the city report that new condo developments are much more likely to have community space. "These amenities are drawing people out of their apartments," says Paula Liebman, president of the Corcoran Group. People living in apartment buildings that have common space for joint recreation seems like a good trend. The article also quotes Dalton Conley, chairman of the NYU department of sociology, reminding us that people in poorer neighborhoods have always used parks, stoops, and city-run pools for meeting neighbors. He adds, "I do think this possibly is new to these folks [affluent apartment-dwellers] who have traditionally used economic power to buy privacy and individual anonymity." That is exactly why we think this news item is important. The long-standing link between high status and stepping back may be breaking down. Here are folks using economic power to buy the chance to see their neighbors at breakfast!

An AARP study of women over forty-five finds a parallel movement in ideas about desirable living arrangements.[2] Thirty-nine percent say that if they were alone, they would find the idea of sharing a home with women friends to be appealing. Unlike the New York breakfasts, these desires do not signal a change in the high status of privacy. These women are returning to traditional reasons for not living alone. Almost all of them (89 percent) say that companionship is the major appeal, but saving money is just as important (85 percent), along with safety (80 percent), and help in medical emergencies (79 percent). Nonetheless, if these women follow through on their wishes in significant numbers, it will have a major impact on the amount of one-person households.

Community service has become a more regular part of the curriculum for high-school students and is spreading exponentially into college and beyond, with young people working in and starting nonprofits at an astounding rate. There are upward of five thousand nonprofits in the Boston area alone. Many of these organizations duplicate services already offered by others, but they give young people who are deciding where to put their energy after college opportunities that were previously not on the table. A good example of a nongovernmental organization that seems to be leading to long-term changes in its volunteers' sense of community is Teach for America. It is highly competitive, and young people feel honored when they are accepted to teach in underserved areas of the country. The program remains controversial. A friend of ours condemned it for "injecting into schools teachers who will leave after a few years to chase more lucrative professions." The evidence from Teach for America's own surveys suggests a more positive outcome. After their time in Teach for America, a very large number of volunteers remain involved in both public education and community service.[3] They also remain engaged with one another, much as Peace Corps volunteers did in an earlier generation. After all, intense shared experiences and an ongoing shared commitment to improving public education is just the sort of thing that leads people to talk to one another regularly about "matters of importance." The long-term effects of programs like Teach for America on social capital may be similar to those of the settlement house movement a century ago. Here is Robert Putnam's description of those effects:

> Settlement houses made valuable contributions to the lives of the urban poor... Ironically, however, the most significant long-term effect of the settlement house movement was not on the recipients of service, but on the service givers... The range of leaders who came out of the experience of settlement houses was extraordinary—not merely scores of social reformers... but also future public-spirited business magnates.[4]

A dramatically different example of a natural corrective to drifting apart is the new Internet site CouchSurfing.com, "an on-line network of travelers, mostly in their twenties, who are tired of staying in hotels and hostels and who want to see the world with a free place to crash—often on someone's couch."[5] The goal is not just cheap lodgings but human connection. The group checks on its results and reports nearly 240,000 friendships formed among it 285,000 registered users. So there are some hopeful signs, including uses of technology to support rather than replace face-to-face human engagement. These naturally developing correctives to social isolation make awareness and education much easier to achieve. People are most likely to make different choices when they understand a problem in a new way and can see good examples of better choices that are out there already.

Politics

In recent years, social fragmentation has emerged as a political issue as well. Political remedies have been proposed, most notably by communitarian writers like Amitai Etzioni. We will leave most of the arguments about political policy to politicians and pundits, but we are willing to risk a few comments.

We begin by repeating Skinner's wisdom in a slightly different form. Policies that support naturally occurring social networks are likely to work better than attempts to create social networks. Removing obstacles to connection is the best way to harness the natural reinforcers of social engagement, that is, the dopamine-mediated pleasures of attachment that are built into human biology. Chief among the obstacles is the frenetic pace of the twenty-first-century workplace and the length of the workday and workweek. It deprives people of time for social lives and it drains them of the energy to make those social lives happen. The Family and Medical Leave Act of 1993 is an example of a policy decision that removed certain obstacles to family connections for at least some Americans. Other measures are certainly possible, but we are not at all qualified to judge the arguments about their impact on employment rates and global competitiveness. We are, however, clear that greater flexibility in work hours would be a boon to families and communities. Robert Putnam's data "point[s] unambiguously to the civic as well as personal dividends associated with part-time employment...We found that part-time workers are typically more involved in community activities than *either* full-time employees *or* people who are not employed at all."[6] These findings suggest that with just a little room to breathe, many people would choose to be more socially involved.

These findings also echo a conclusion we came to twenty-five years ago, in a small study of the effect that a woman's employment level has on marriage. When women worked part-time while their children were young, both partners were happier with the marriage, and the husbands were more involved with their children, than when women either worked full-time or were stay-at-home mothers.[7] We suspect that the effect of a wife's part-time employment on her husband's level of involvement with their children reflects a more general phenomenon. If one member of a couple has the flexibility of part-time work, the family as a whole is likely to be much more socially engaged. When both partners are working full-time (and in present-day America, full-time usually means much more than the traditional forty-hour week), there is no one to mind the social calendar, and connections start to fray.

Other than employment policies and tax proposals that are intended to support marriage and families, the area that has generated the most proposals for the renewal of community life is urban design and architecture—an attempt to understand how the physical structures of small-town life enhance community connections and then to adapt those structures to new urban and suburban settings. It seems to us that many of the proposals that have emerged from this approach must be viewed as experiments, filled with interesting possibilities but no certainties. We live in a part of Cambridge, Massachusetts, that is enough of a mixed-use community to allow us regularly to encounter friends in local stores or while running errands on foot. The houses are close together, so neighbors frequently see one another coming and going. Friends who have moved back in town from more leafy and car-centered suburbs (usually after their children have left home) talk about the very different feeling created by the differences in physical layout. We believe that urban design has powerful effects on the nature of a community. On the other hand, it is hard to be sure which elements are the most important. We were intrigued by a proposal to give tax credits for the construction of front porches. The idea was that most American small towns of the past had houses with front porches where people sat, looking outward, seeing neighbors, and keeping track of what went on. Bring back front porches and you bring back community, as well as improve safety. It was such a simple and elegant idea that we were immediately taken with it. Yet when we were strolling through our neighborhood not long ago, we noticed that there are a fair number of front porches, and we hardly ever see anyone sitting on them. Now, researchers once found that people in Cambridge were even more hurried in their ordinary activities than people in New York City. We believe that architecture can make a difference, but in our neighborhood, culture and ambition have trumped architecture in at least one head-to-head contest.

Religion

No discussion of human connection can afford to ignore the importance of religion. Harvard psychiatrist George Vaillant once summarized the time course of various human organizations. The average Fortune 500 company lasts several decades; a family dynasty several generations; nation-states several hundred years. The only organizations in human history that have survived more than a thousand years are religious organizations. Vaillant also quoted the words of one of his college professors, words he'd remembered over most of a lifetime: "If you don't believe that your religion is the one true religion, then you don't have a religion."[8] These two observations, taken together, effectively define the influence of religious affiliation in human affairs. It is the most powerful uniting force in human history, knitting together individuals and groups into large, interconnected communities. It is also the most powerful divisive force in human history, shattering communities with unrivaled violence. Religion will clearly continue to play a major role in American connectedness, and it will continue to be a source of rich social networks *within* religious groups. What role it will play in relationships *among* groups, whether it will enhance connection or cause separation, is at this moment very uncertain.

One thing is certain. Religious life speaks directly to the discontents that arise from a socially disconnected life, and it offers a cure. Remember that the cognitive effects of social exclusion include meaninglessness and lethargy. A welcoming pastor and a welcoming congregation solve the problem of social exclusion and at the same time offer direct relief from meaninglessness and lethargy. The dramatic rise of membership in evangelical churches over the last several decades is no doubt a response to a complicated mix of yearnings, but the yearning for *human* connection has played a major role. Some of the more successful churches are very clear on this point and have explicitly organized themselves into just the kind of small groups that are best at making lonely individuals feel connected and held, the kind of small group that formed the basic survival strategy of the human species. We are "built" to need and to respond to the connection and holding that small groups provide. The question now (and throughout human history) is whether the connection to "our" group requires a corresponding sense of "others" as enemies. If the small group is the basic survival strategy of the human species, a sense of us-against-them naturally comes along as part of the package. Most major religions have, at the core of their teachings, a wider embrace that counters the us-against-them tendencies in human nature. Most major religions have also, at crucial moments in history, fanned the flames of us-against-them sentiments, with murderous consequences. We can only hope.

According to Robert Putnam, the current data on religion and social networks is not encouraging:

> As the twenty-first century opens, Americans are going to church less than we did three or four decades ago, and the churches we go to are less engaged with the wider community. Trends in religious life reinforce rather than counterbalance the ominous plunge in social connectedness in the secular community.[9]

Yet religious life and religious organizations remain a vital source of social connectedness in the personal lives of individuals. Even if religion is not currently the wellspring of social capital that it once was in America, it still plays a major role in countering the social isolation of individuals and families. To us as clinicians, that is no small point.

Environment

Contemplating the steady increase in one-person households over the last half a century, both here and in Western Europe, we reviewed British research on its ecological consequences. The short summary is that the rise of one-person households significantly increases resource consumption, energy use, and waste production. A shorter summary is a headline from the *Guardian Unlimited*: "Solo Living's Eco Threat." Part of the issue is simply the economics of sharing. When homes are shared, a whole array of resources are also automatically shared. Sharing resources reduces humanity's impact on the environment.

There is another process at work here that multiplies the environmental impact of social isolation far beyond the simple economics of sharing. Across all age groups, people living alone are far more likely to spend money on themselves than people in other living arrangements. Social isolation itself increases the use of consumer goods as a source of comfort and satisfaction. Remember the dopaminergic reward system in the brain. It lights up with love and with cocaine. It also lights up with shopping.

The authors can vouch for that with their own brains. Each one of us remembers (separately) coping with lonely moments in college by ambling off to the college bookstore to buy records. The physical realities of living alone create physical needs that increase consumption. The emotional realities of social isolation create emotional needs that also increase consumption. The effect of both is to increase per capita environmental impact.

Here is an area where urban design, architecture, and zoning policies can make a difference, developing and expanding models of living arrangements that offer people some of the freedom of solo living while reducing its profligate use of limited resources. One example is co-housing, an intriguing mix of independent and community living. People have their own private apartments, but both community space and community activities (including meals together several times each week) are designed into the plan. The approach began in Europe, and there are now several small developments in the Boston area. On a recent trip to the local post office, we ran into friends of ours, an elderly couple (they are now well into their eighties) who had left their single-family home about ten years ago to move into a co-housing development nearby. They could not have been more enthusiastic about their experience. It has allowed them to adjust the balance of independence and connection in ways that they feel has worked wonderfully. At the same time, co-housing (in the words of a British researcher) "increases space, energy and goods savings."[10] No living arrangement will ever be right for everybody, but at least for some people, co-housing lets them have their cake and eat it too. They can be independent but not lonely, and they can be happy but still decrease their environmental footprint. There must be many other arrangements that balance the desires for both separateness and connection, waiting to be created with just a little encouragement (and financing). Not all the ideas will require different approaches to building and arranging houses. Even small social innovations like shared breakfasts in New York condos, which leave the physical demands of solo living on the world's resources unchanged, can still make a difference by reducing loneliness-driven consumption.

Automobile use is not a bad analogy. The ecological consequences of solo living are similar to the ecological consequences of solo driving. It is the stationary version of the same problem. A two-pronged response that includes technological innovation (to improve the efficiency of solo living) and the development of appealing alternatives (like co-housing) would mirror well-established strategies in transportation (improving fuel efficiency of cars, encouraging carpooling and mass transit). A rush-hour drive in any big city, with streets and highways clogged with cars that mostly have just one person in each of them, also makes clear the challenges involved. Awareness of a problem, education about its consequences, and innovations that make alternatives easier and more appealing are all linked together in a process that, over time, can shift the choices that individuals make.

Heroes

Easier *and* more appealing are not always joined together in the same choice. Most people seek more than just the easiest path. In the end, we as a nation must return to the ideals that shape the choices we make—the myths that we live by and the heroes of those myths in whose footsteps we long to follow. We need our lonesome heroes, standing apart but ready to step in and save the town when the time comes, supplying the courage or the creativity that grows wild only on the frontier. We also need other heroes, those whose courage and creativity flow from their engagement and connection with others rather than from their apartness. Our history and our stories are filled with those other heroes, but the spotlight has not shone on them quite as brightly.

Fifteen years ago, William Kilpatrick, a professor of education at Boston College, offered both a description and a name for these other heroes. He called them *ordinary heroes.* His subject was how children learn moral values. He argued that morality was taught best through stories, heroic stories. At some point, however, the heroes of childhood stop working for most adults, and a more mature understanding of heroism is required. Part of the difference for Kilpatrick is the hero's degree of social connectedness. He writes:

For the traditional hero . . . the adventure takes place away from home. Home is where you go after the adventure; it is essentially the end of the adventure. For the average hero, on the other hand, home *is* the adventure, the place where he lays himself on the line. *The adventure consists precisely in those commitments with which the classical hero or child hero rarely allows himself to be entangled* [italics ours]. The temptation for the traditional hero is to avoid the adventure and settle down; the temptation for the ordinary hero is to avoid commitment and have an adventure.[11]

Kilpatrick wants us (as adults) to celebrate the heroism of commitment, attachment, social engagement. He offers the figure of George Bailey in Frank Capra's film *It's a Wonderful Life* as a superb example of the "heroism of sustained commitment."[12] In our terms, it is the heroism of not stepping back.

Great ideals can be used to hide ordinary failings. The inspiring ideal of the self-reliant outsider can supply a heroic gloss for a decision to give up on relationships, with all their difficulties, demands, and complications. It lets us spin an escape as an act of courage. Not that we don't all need our moments of escape. But if we sell ourselves on the idea that our escapes ennoble us, we are much less likely to find our way back. And if we have stories about staying engaged that can also make us feel brave, if we include in our pantheon of heroes individuals who step into the fray of human entanglements, then we enhance both our awareness of the choices we make and our freedom to choose. We become more limber, more responsive to the realities of our circumstances. We start to free the small but crucial decisions of everyday life from a set of glorious but too-rigid ideals that have not always served us well.

We as a nation reach for just a little more freedom, a little peace and quiet, a little more space to breathe and move. *The Pur-*

suit of Loneliness is the name that Philip Slater gave to his book about social disconnection in America, but loneliness was never really the goal. The story we have to tell about American loneliness is ultimately a story about the pursuit of happiness, a search for a little respite and dignity in a frenetic world. Loneliness is not the goal. It's just the spot where too many people wind up. The solution to the problem of social disconnection in America is not to eradicate moments of solitude in people's lives. The solution is not even to eliminate moments of loneliness in people's lives—they are part of the human condition. At times they are even a restorative part of the human condition. Leon Wieseltier, in a journal of meditation and study that he kept during the year after his father's death, wrote, "I walked . . . to the old stone bench near the bottom of the hill at the far edge of the gardens. For years I have been coming to this bench for a little loneliness."[13] There are times in all of our lives when we each need a little loneliness. There are times when loneliness has something important to teach us. Without it, how can we cherish our attachments and pay our respects to the ones that we lose? It comes down to a question of balance. Aristotle was no fool when he equated virtue with the golden mean. As a country, we have lost our balance. It is so easy for each of us to seek out an old stone bench at the far edge of the garden, where a little loneliness awaits, and then get stuck there. We get stuck because the world we have wandered away from is so frantic and demanding. We get stuck because we have dreamed about loner-heroes who sit (and stand) apart. We get stuck because we feel left out and soon stop looking for ways back in. We should remember, both as individuals and as a society, that the bench was not meant to be our final destination.

Acknowledgments

We have been helped in this project by many people. We particularly want to thank Christine Cipriani, formerly of Beacon Press, for initially proposing a book on the subject and shepherding it through its early stages, and Amy Caldwell, for so ably taking over as our editor in midstream. We appreciate the careful copyediting of Tracy Roe. Maggie and Craig McEwen helped us clarify and deepen our ideas about outsiders just as we were starting to develop them. Sarah and Nathaniel Schwartz, James Leland Olds, and Sherry Turkle gave us valuable feedback on specific chapters. Peter Rogers and Carol Sacerdote helped clarify certain important points and sharpen our writing. Robert Putnam was generous in allowing us to read a prepublication version of ongoing research. Peter Bearman and Paolo Parigi were kind enough to provide us with unpublished data from their study of social connection. And Jamie Delson graced us with his incomparable knowledge of Westerns.

Notes

Chapter 1: The Elephant in the Room

1. Miller McPherson, Lynn Smith-Lovin, and Matthew E. Brashears, "Social Isolation in America: Changes in Core Discussion Networks over Two Decades," *American Sociological Review* 71 (June 2006): 353–75.

2. U.S. Bureau of the Census, "Historical Census of Housing Tables: Living Alone," December 2004, www.census.gov/hhes/www/housing/census/historic/livalone.html.

3. Philip Slater, *The Pursuit of Loneliness: American Culture at the Breaking Point* (Boston: Beacon Press, 1970), 5.

4. Jeffrey Boase, John B. Horrigan, Barry Wellman, and Lee Rainie, *The Strength of Internet Ties* (Washington, DC: Pew Internet and American Life Project, 2006), www.pewinternet.org/pdfs/PIP-Internet-ties.pdf. Specific data on core and close ties is on p. 6.

5. McPherson, Smith-Lovin, and Brashears, "Social Isolation."

6. Another research group from Columbia University, using data similar to the GSS, looked very carefully at the "silent group" that reported not discussing important matters with anyone. Forty-four percent said they had no one to talk to, and 56 percent said they had nothing of importance to talk about. (Peter Bearman and Paolo Parigi, "Cloning Headless Frogs, and Other Important Matters: Conversation Topic and Network Structure," *Social Forces* 83 [2004]: 535–37.) The categories

seem clear, but we think they are misleading. Often it is only in dialogue with another human being that a topic starts to achieve importance.

7. Alexis de Tocqueville, *Democracy in America*, ed. Phillips Bradley (1835; reprint New York: A. A. Knopf, 1945), 106–7. Citations are from the Knopf edition.

Chapter 2: Frantic without a Peep

1. Elizabeth Warren and Amelia Warren Tyagi, *The Two-Income Trap: Why Middle-Class Mothers and Fathers Are Going Broke* (New York: Basic Books, 2003), 51–52, 208.

2. Barbara Ehrenreich, *The Worst Years of Our Lives: Irreverent Notes from a Decade of Greed* (New York: Pantheon, 1990), 22–25.

3. Juliet B. Schor, *The Overworked American: The Unexpected Decline of Leisure* (New York: Basic Books, 1992), 28–32.

4. Michael Hout and Caroline Hanley, "The Overworked American Family: Trends and Nontrends in Working Hours, 1968–2001," the Survey Research Center, University of California, Berkeley, http://ucdata .berkeley.edu/rsfcensus.

5. Ibid.

6. Al Gini, *The Importance of Being Lazy: In Praise of Play, Leisure, and Vacations* (New York: Routledge, 2003), 16.

7. Timothy Egan, "The Rise of the Shrinking-Vacation Syndrome," *New York Times*, August 20, 2006.

8. Allison Pearson, quoted in "Author Talk," Bookreporter.com (May 2003), www.bookreporter.com/authors/talk-pearson-allison.asp.

9. Jacqueline Olds, Richard S. Schwartz, Susan V. Eisen, R. William Betcher, Anthony Van Niel, "Part-Time Employment and Marital Well-Being: A Hypothesis and Pilot Study," *Family Therapy* 20 (1993): 1–16.

Chapter 3: Self-Reliance

1. Ralph Waldo Emerson, "Self-Reliance," in *The Complete Writings of Ralph Waldo Emerson*, vol. 1 (New York: Wm. H. Wise and Co., 1930), 138–44.

2. The *Star Wars* phenomenon, with its decades-long run, is the most obvious heir to the Westerns of the mid-twentieth century, but the Western's loner-hero mystique turns up in all sorts of seemingly non-Western

vehicles. We find it in expected places like the 2007 movie *Shooter* ("the movie celebrates [the protagonist's] prowess in all its solitary cultic glory," said David Denby in his column "Men Gone Wild" in the April 2, 2007, edition of *The New Yorker*). And we also find it in new guises, perhaps most clearly in the burgeoning industry of vampire-themed narratives, which includes Anne Rice's extremely popular vampire novels and the cult TV series *Buffy the Vampire Slayer*.

3. "Interview with Howard Hawks: Peter Bogdanovich/1962," in *Howard Hawks: Interviews*, ed. Scott Brievold (Jackson: University Press of Mississippi, 2006), 37.

4. Todd McCarthy, *Howard Hawks: The Grey Fox of Hollywood* (New York: Grove Press, 1997), 548–49.

5. Robert N. Bellah, "Flaws in the Protestant Code: Theological Roots of American Individualism," in *The Robert Bellah Reader*, eds. Robert N. Bellah and Steven M. Tipton (Durham, NC: Duke University Press, 2006), 345.

6. Jacqueline Olds, Richard Schwartz, and Harriet Webster, *Overcoming Loneliness in Everyday Life* (New York: Birch Lane Press, 1996), 26–27.

7. Mary Midgley, *Can't We Make Moral Judgements?* (New York: St. Martin's Press, 1991), 111.

8. Charles A. Reich, *The Greening of America* (New York: Bantam Books, 1971), 251–57.

9. Jack Hitt, "The Amateur Future of Space Travel," *New York Times Magazine*, July 1, 2007.

10. Ron Suskind, "Nickolas C. Murnion," in *Profiles in Courage for Our Time*, ed. Caroline Kennedy (New York: Hyperion, 2002), 175.

11. David Brooks, "The New Lone Rangers," *New York Times*, July 10, 2007.

12. Quoted in Roger Lowenstein, "Off the Shelf: He Didn't Mean to Make a Fortune, But Oh Well...," *New York Times*, August 8, 2006.

13. Sigmund Freud, "The Neuro-Psychoses of Defense (1)," in *The Standard Edition of the Complete Psychological Works of Sigmund Freud*, ed. James Strachey (London: Hogarth Press, 1962), 59.

14. The artist as outsider reminds us that the outsider myth is not entirely made in America. A European version was articulated best by the

Englishman Colin Wilson in his book *The Outsider* (1956; reprint New York: Jeremy P. Tarcher/Putnam, 1982), which became an underground classic. Without the American tradition of strong individualism and a frontier in which that spirit could be expressed in action, Wilson's outsider hero is a more cerebral creature, an artist or intellectual who, standing apart, is able to see the Truth (his capitalization). Wilson's outsider is no adventure hero. His case "is weakened by his obvious abnormality, his introversion" (Wilson, *The Outsider*, 14). Wilson's emphasis on the "strangeness" of his outsiders, including their own uneasiness with themselves, stands in marked contrast to a certain brilliant-but-regular-guy tone cultivated by American Transcendentalists such as Emerson and Thoreau. Wilson's vision is distinctly less comforting to those of us who find ourselves inadvertently alone and apart. It might be a bracing tonic, but it's no spoonful of sugar.

15. Jo Blanden, Paul Gregg, and Stephen Machin, "Intergenerational Mobility in Europe and North America," Centre for Economic Performance, April 2005, http://cep.lse.ac.uk/about/news/Intergenerational Mobility.pdf.

16. John Mack Faragher, "Open-Country Community: Sugar Creek, Illinois, 1820–1850," in *The Countryside in the Age of Capitalistic Transformation*, eds. Steven Hahn and Jonathan Prude (Chapel Hill: University of North Carolina Press, 1985), 245.

17. John Mack Faragher, *Sugar Creek: Life on the Illinois Prairie* (New Haven: Yale University Press, 1986), 132–33.

18. Susan Cheever, *American Bloomsbury* (New York: Simon and Schuster, 2006), 6.

19. Pauline Maier, in a conversation with the authors about fourteen years ago.

20. Quoted in Linda Matchen, "Is This the Home of the Future?" *Boston Globe*, January 25, 2007.

21. Robin Wood, *Rio Bravo* (London: British Film Institute Publishing, 2003), 12.

22. Frederick Jackson Turner, "The Significance of the Frontier in American History," American Historical Association Web site, www.historians.org/pubs/archives/Turnerthesis.htm.

Chapter 4: Left Out

1. Patricia R. Barchas, "A Sociophysiological Orientation to Small Groups," *Advances in Group Processes*, vol. 3, ed. Edward J. Lawler (Greenwich, CT: JAI Press, 1986), 212.

2. Steven Pinker, *The Blank Slate: The Modern Denial of Human Nature* (New York: Penguin Books, 2002), 258.

3. Robin Dunbar, *Grooming, Gossip and the Evolution of Language* (London: Faber and Faber, 1996), 1–77.

4. Andreas Bartels and Semir Zeki, "The Neural Basis of Romantic Love," *NeuroReport* 11 (November 27, 2000): 3829–34.

5. Andreas Bartels and Semir Zeki, "The Neural Correlates of Maternal and Romantic Love," *NeuroImage* 21 (2004): 1155–66.

6. J. W. Howard and M. Rothbart, "Social Categorization and Memory for In-group and Out-group Behavior," *Journal of Personality and Social Psychology* 38 (1980): 301–10.

7. Donelson R. Forsyth and Barry R. Schlenker, "Attributing the Causes of Group Performance: Effects of Performance Quality, Task Importance, and Future Testing," *Journal of Personality* 45 (1977): 220–36.

8. Thomas R. Insel, "Is Social Attachment an Addictive Disorder?," *Physiology and Behavior* 79 (2003): 351–57.

9. Paul MacLean, *The Triune Brain in Evolution: Role in Paleocerebral Functions* (New York: Plenum, 1990), 380–411.

10. C. S. Carter, "Biological Perspectives on Social Attachment and Bonding," in *Attachment and Bonding: A New Synthesis*, eds. C. S. Carter, L. Ahnert, K. E. Grossmann, S. B. Hrdy, M. E. Lamb, S. W. Porges, and N. Sachser (Cambridge, MA: MIT Press, 2005), 85–100.

11. J. K. Kiecolt-Glaser, L. D. Fisher, P. Ogrocki, et al., "Marital Quality, Marital Disruption, and Immune Function," *Psychosomatic Medicine* 49 (1987): 13–32.

12. Michael B. Hennessy, "Hypothalamic-Pituitary-Adrenal Responses to Brief Social Separations," *Neuroscience and Biobehavioral Reviews* 21 (1996): 11–29.

13. Ibid.

14. Jean M. Twenge, Roy F. Baumeister, Dianne M. Tice, and Tanja

S. Stucke, "If You Can't Join Them, Beat Them: Effects of Social Exclusion on Aggressive Behavior," *Journal of Personality and Social Psychology* 81 (2001): 1058–69.

15. Ibid.

16. Jean M. Twenge, Kathleen R. Catanes, and Roy F. Baumeister, "Social Exclusion Causes Self-Defeating Behavior," *Journal of Personality and Social Psychology* 83 (2002): 606–15.

17. Roy F. Baumeister, Jean M. Twenge, and Christopher K. Nuss, "Effects of Social Exclusion on Cognitive Processes: Anticipated Aloneness Reduces Intelligent Thought," *Journal of Personality and Social Psychology* 83 (2002): 817–27.

18. Jean M. Twenge, Kathleen R. Catanes, and Roy F. Baumeister, "Social Exclusion and the Deconstructed State: Time Perception, Meaninglessness, Lethargy, Lack of Emotion, and Self-Awareness," *Journal of Personality and Social Psychology* 85 (2003): 409–23.

19. Roy F. Baumeister, C. Nathan DeWall, Natalie J. Ciarocco, and Jean M. Twenge, "Social Exclusion Impairs Self-Regulation," *Journal of Personality and Social Psychology* 88 (2005): 589–604.

20. Henri Tajfel, M. G. Billig, and R. P. Bundy, "Social Categorization and Intergroup Behavior," *European Journal of Social Psychology* 1 (1971): 149–78.

21. Ricky Susan Stern, "The Politics of Childhood: An Evolutionary View of Childhood Networks as In-groups," *Dissertation Abstracts International: Section B: The Sciences and Engineering* 62 (October 2001): 2097.

Chapter 5: Free at Last

1. U.S. Bureau of the Census, "Historical Census of Housing Tables: Living Alone," December 2004, www.census.gov/hhes/www/housing/census/historic/livalone.html.

2. David B. Caruso, "Census Says Manhattan First in Single-Person Households: Numbers on Rise across the Nation," *Boston Globe*, September 3, 2005.

3. Boston Redevelopment Authority, "For the First Time in Boston's History, Non-Family Households Top 50 Percent," in *Insight: A Briefing Report on a Topic of Current Interest*, May 2002.

4. Philip Slater, *The Pursuit of Loneliness: American Culture at the Breaking Point* (Boston: Beacon Press, 1970), 7.

5. National Agency for Enterprise and Housing, Denmark, *Housing Statistics in the European Union 2003*, www.ebst.dk/file/2256/housing _statistics_2003.pdf.

6. Slater, *Pursuit of Loneliness*, 7.

7. Duane F. Alwin, Philip E. Converse, and Steven S. Martin, "Living Arrangements and Social Integration," *Journal of Marriage and the Family* 47 (1985): 319–34.

8. Miranda Lewis, *Unilever Family Report 2005: Home Alone?* (Unilever and the Institute for Public Policy Research, 2005), www.unilever .co.uk/ourvalues/environmentandsociety/publications/familyreport/.

9. Norman H. Nie and D. Sunshine Hillygus, "The Impact of Internet Use on Sociability: Time-Diary Findings," *IT & Society* 1 (2002): 1–20.

10. Lewis, *Unilever Family Report 2005*.

11. Ibid.

12. Jim Bennet and Mike Dixon, *Single-Person Households and Social Policy: Looking Forwards* (York: Joseph Rowntree Foundation and the Institute for Public Policy Research, 2006), www.jrf.org.uk/bookshop/.

13. Joan Chandler, Malcolm Williams, Moira Maconachie, Tracey Collett, and Brian Dodgeon, "Living Alone: Its Place in Household Formation and Change," *Sociological Research Online* 9 (2004), www.socres online.org,uk/9/3/chandler.html.

14. Lewis, *Unilever Family Report 2005*.

15. Stacey J. Oliker, *Best Friends and Marriage: Exchange Among Women* (Berkeley: University of California Press, 1989), 123.

16. Bennet and Dixon, *Single-Person Households*.

17. Jean M. Twenge, Sara Konrath, Joshua D. Foster, W. Keith Campbell, and Brad J. Bushman, "Egos Inflating Over Time: A Cross-Temporal Meta-Analysis of the Narcissistic Personality Inventory," *Journal of Personality* 76 (2008): 875–902.

18. Ulla G. Foehr, "Media Multitasking Among American Youth: Prevalence, Predictors and Pairings" (Henry J. Kaiser Family Foundation, 2006), www.kff.org/entmedia/upload/7592.pdf.

19. For example, Claude S. Fischer, Robert M. Jackson, Ann Steuve, Katherine Gerson, and Lynn M. Jones, *Networks and Places: Social Relations in the Urban Setting* (New York: Free Press, 1977), 39–58.

20. Wendell Berry, *Jayber Crow* (Washington, DC: Counterpoint, 2000), 72.

21. Mihaly Csikszentmihalyi, *Flow: The Psychology of Optimal Experience* (New York: Harper and Row, 1990), 157–73.

22. John Updike, *Rabbit Is Rich* (New York: Fawcett Columbine, 1996), 419.

23. Jo Williams, quoted in Charlotte Moore, "Solo Living's Eco Threat," *Guardian Unlimited*, August 1, 2006.

24. Jo Williams, "Innovative Solutions for Averting a Potential Resource Crisis—the Case of One-Person Households in England and Wales," *Environment, Development and Sustainability* 9 (2007): 325–54.

25. Moore, "Solo Living's Eco Threat."

26. "One Is Fun—and Lucrative Too," *Food&DrinkEurope.com*, July 4, 2003, www.foodanddrinkeurope.com.

27. James Morrow, "A Place for One," *American Demographics*, November 1, 2003.

28. Ibid.

Chapter 6: The Technology of Relationships

1. Jeffrey Boase, John B. Horrigan, Barry Wellman, and Lee Rainie, *The Strength of Internet Ties* (Washington, DC: Pew Internet and American Life Project, 2006), i.

2. Norman H. Nie and Lutz Erbring, "Internet and Society: A Preliminary Report," *IT & Society* 1 (2002): 275–83.

3. Norman H. Nie. and D. Sunshine Hillygus, "The Impact of Internet Use on Sociability: Time-Diary Findings," *IT & Society* 1 (2002): 1–20.

4. Ulla G. Foehr, "Media Multitasking Among American Youth: Prevalence, Predictors and Pairings" (Henry J. Kaiser Family Foundation, 2006), www.kff.org/entmedia/upload/7592.pdf.

5. Maura Welch, "The Fast Eat the Slow," *Boston Globe*, May 28, 2007.

6. Daniel Goleman, "Flame First, Think Later: New Clues to E-Mail Misbehavior," *New York Times*, February 20, 2007.

7. Jennifer S. Beer, Oliver P. John, Donatella Scabini, and Robert T. Knight, "Orbitofrontal Cortex and Social Behavior: Integrating Self-monitoring and Emotional–Cognition Interactions," *Journal of Cognitive Neuroscience* 18 (2006): 871–879.

8. Morten L. Kringelback and Edmund T. Rolls, "The Functional Neuroanatomy of the Human Orbitofrontal Cortex: Evidence from Neuroimaging and Neuropsychology," *Progress in Neurobiology* 72 (2004): 341–72.

9. Goleman, "Flame First."

10. Johann Wolfgang von Goethe, on listening to J. S. Bach, quoted in Pierre Tristam, "Passion of the Johann: An All-Bach Christmas," *Daytona Beach News-Journal*, December 20, 2005.

11. Daniel J. Levitin, *This Is Your Brain on Music: The Science of a Human Obsession* (New York: Dutton, 2006), 5–6.

12. Bradley W. Vines, Carol L. Krumhansl, Marcelo M. Wanderley, and Daniel J. Levitin, "Cross-modal Interactions in the Perception of Musical Performance," *Cognition* 101 (2006): 80–113.

13. Clive Thompson, "Music of the Hemispheres," *New York Times*, December 31, 2006.

14. Timothy Egan, "Erotica, Inc.—a Special Report: Technology Sent Wall Street into Market for Pornography," *New York Times*, October 23, 2000.

15. John Tierney, "Romantic Revulsion in the New Century: Flaw-O-Matic 2.0," *New York Times*, April 10, 2007.

16. Barry Schwartz, "The Tyranny of Choice," *Scientific American* (April 2004): 70–75.

17. Sherry Turkle, "Always-On/Always-On-You: The Tethered Self," in *Handbook of Mobile Communication Studies*, ed. James Katz (Cambridge, MA: MIT Press, 2008).

Chapter 7: Love and Marriage in a Busy World

1. Miller McPherson, Lynn Smith-Lovin, and Matthew E. Brashears, "Social Isolation in America: Changes in Core Discussion Networks over Two Decades," *American Sociological Review* 71 (June 2006): 353–75.

2. The numbers are a bit confusing. The GSS found that the percentage of respondents who identified a spouse as a confidant increased from about 30 percent in 1985 to 38 percent in 2004, but the percentages are for all respondents, not just those who are married.

3. Theodore Caplow, Howard M. Bahr, Bruce A. Chadwick, R. Hill,

and M. H. Williamson, *The Middletown Families: Fifty Years of Continuity and Change* (Minneapolis: University of Minnesota Press, 1982), 117.

4. Lynn Smith-Lovin, *On Point*, National Public Radio, June 28, 2006.

5. Jacqueline Olds, Richard S. Schwartz, Susan V. Eisen, R. William Betcher, and Anthony Van Niel, "Part-Time Employment and Marital Well-Being: A Hypothesis and Pilot Study," *Family Therapy* 20 (1993): 1–16.

6. Stacey Oliker, *Best Friends and Marriage: Exchange Among Women* (Berkeley: University of California Press, 1989), 57.

7. Naomi Gerstel and Natalia Sarkisian, "The Good, the Bad, and the Greedy," *Contexts* 5 (2006): 16–21.

8. Stephanie Coontz, "Too Close for Comfort," *New York Times*, November 7, 2006.

9. Suzanne M. Bianchi, John P. Robinson, and Melissa A. Milkie, *Changing Rhythms of American Family Life* (New York: Russell Sage Foundation, 2006).

10. Pamela Druckerman, *Lust in Translation: The Rules of Infidelity from Tokyo to Tennessee* (New York: Penguin Press, 2007), 180.

11. Hara Estroff Marano and Shirley Glass, "Shattered Vows: Getting Beyond Betrayal," *Psychology Today* (July–August 1998).

12. Philip Cowan and Caroline Pape Cowan, "New Families: Modern Couples as New Pioneers," in *All Our Families: New Policies for a New Century*, eds. Mary Ann Mason, Arlene Skolnick, and Stephen D. Sugarman (New York: Oxford University Press, 2003), 196–219.

13. E. H. Newberger, R. L. Hampton, T. J. Marx, and K. M. White, "Child Abuse and Pediatric Social Illness: An Epidemiological Analysis and Ecological Reformulation," *American Journal of Orthopsychiatry* 56 (1986): 589–601.

14. David Popenoe and Barbara Dafoe Whitehead, "The State of Our Unions: The Social Health of Marriage in America, 1999," National Marriage Project, http://marriage.rutgers.edu.

15. Peter Bearman and Paolo Parigi, "Cloning Headless Frogs, and Other Important Matters: Conversation Topic and Network Structure," *Social Forces* 83 (2004): 535–37.

16. E. Kay Trimberger, *The New Single Woman* (Boston: Beacon Press, 2007), 19.

17. Sam Roberts, "To Be Married Means to Be Outnumbered," *New York Times*, October 15, 2006.

18. David Popenoe and Barbara Dafoe Whitehead, "The State of Our Unions: The Social Health of Marriage in America, 2007," National Marriage Project, http://marriage.rutgers.edu.

19. Richard Schwartz and Jacqueline Olds, *Marriage in Motion: The Natural Ebb and Flow of Lasting Relationships* (Cambridge, MA: Perseus Publishing, 2000), 118.

20. Robert D. Putnam, *Bowling Alone: The Collapse and Revival of American Community* (New York: Touchstone, 2000), 100.

Chapter 8: The Ripple Effects of Increasing Social Isolation

1. B. N. Uchino, J. T. Cacioppo, and J. K. Kiecolt-Glaser, "The Relationship between Social Support and Physiological Processes: A Review with Emphasis on Underlying Mechanisms and Implications for Health," *Psychological Bulletin* 119 (1996): 488–531; Richard S. Schwartz and Jacqueline Olds, "Loneliness," *Harvard Review of Psychiatry* 5 (1997): 94–98; Jacqueline Olds, Richard S. Schwartz, and Harriet Webster, "The Hazards of Loneliness," in *Overcoming Loneliness in Everyday Life* (New York: Birch Lane, 1996), 32–47; J. S. House, K. R. Landis, and D. Umberson, "Social Relationships and Health," *Science* 241 (1988): 540–45; Stewart Wolf and John G. Bruhn, *The Power of the Clan: The Influence of Human Relationships on Heart Disease* (New Brunswick, NJ: Transaction Publishers, 1993); Laura Fratiglioni, Hui-Xin Wang, Kjerstin Ericsson, Margaret Mayton, and Bengt Winblad, "Influence of Social Networks on Occurrence of Dementia: Community-Based Longitudinal Study," *Lancet* 355 (2000): 1315–19.

2. J. F. Lechman, rapporteur, C. S. Carter, M. B. Hennessy, S. B. Hrdy, E. B. Keverne, G. Klann-Delius, C. Schradin, D. Todt, and D. von Holst, "Group Report: Biobehavioral Processes in Attachment and Bonding," in *Attachment and Bonding: A New Synthesis*, eds. C. S. Carter, L. Ahnert, K. E. Grossmann, S. B. Hrdy, M. E. Lamb, S. W. Porges, and N. Sachser (Cambridge, MA: MIT Press, 2005), 337.

3. Steve W. Cole, Louise C. Hawkley, Jesusa M. Arevalo, Caroline Y. Sung, Robert M. Rose, and John T. Cacioppo, "Social Regulation of Gene Expression in Human Leukocytes," *Genome Biology* 8 (2007): R189.

4. "Why Loneliness May Damage Health," BBC News, September 12, 2007,p http://news.bbc.co.uk.

5. Robert D. Putnam, *Making Democracy Work: Civic Traditions in Modern Italy* (Princeton, NJ: Princeton University Press, 1993), 183.

6. James Surowiecki, "The Financial Page: Feature Presentation," *New Yorker,* May 28, 2007.

7. Al Gini, *The Importance of Being Lazy: In Praise of Play, Leisure, and Vacations* (New York: Routledge, 2003), 72.

8. Deborah Shatin and Carol R. Drinkard, "Ambulatory Use of Psychotropics by Employer-Insured Children and Adolescents in a National Managed Care Organization," *Ambulatory Pediatrics* 2 (2002): 111–19.

9. Bureau of Justice Statistics, "Crime and Victims Statistics," U.S. Department of Justice, www.ojp.usdoj.gov/bjs/cvict.htm.

10. E. H. Newberger, R. L. Hampton, T. J. Marx, and K. M. White, "Child Abuse and Pediatric Social Illness: An Epidemiological Analysis and Ecological Reformulation," *American Journal of Orthopsychiatry* 56 (1986): 589–601.

11. Patricia A. Zaradic and Oliver R. W. Pergams, "Videophilia: Implications for Childhood Development and Conservation," *Journal of Developmental Processes* 2 (2007): 130–47.

12. Robert D. Putnam, "E Pluribus Unum: Diversity and Community in the Twenty-First Century: The 2006 Johan Skytte Prize Lecture," *Scandinavian Political Studies* 30 (2007): 137–74.

13. David Brooks, "Closing of a Nation," *New York Times,* July 6, 2007.

14. Jean M. Twenge, Roy F. Baumeister, Dianne M. Tice, and Tanja S. Stucke, "If You Can't Join Them, Beat Them: Effects of Social Exclusion on Aggressive Behavior," *Journal of Personality and Social Psychology* 81 (2001): 1058–69.

15. David Lester, "Time-Series Studies of the Murder and Homicide Rates in the USA," *Perceptual and Motor Skills* 79 (October 1994): 862.

16. Twenge, Baumeister, "If You Can't Join Them."

17. M. D. Resnick, P. S. Bearman, R. Blum, et al., "Protecting Ado-

lescents from Harm: Findings from the National Longitudinal Study on Adolescent Health," *Journal of the American Medical Association* 278 (1997): 823–32.

18. James J. Lynch, *A Cry Unheard: New Insights into the Medical Consequences of Loneliness* (Baltimore: Bancroft Press, 2000), 119–90.

19. Seldon D. Bacon, "Alcohol and Complex Society," in *Society, Culture, and Drinking Patterns*, eds. David J. Pittman and Charles R. Snyder (New York: John Wiley and Sons, 1962), 78–93.

20. Walter R. Gove and Michael Hughes, "Reexamining the Ecological Fallacy: A Study in Which Aggregate Data Are Critical in Investigating the Pathological Effects of Living Alone," *Social Forces* 58 (1980): 1157–77.

21. David G. Blanchflower and Andrew J. Oswald, "Well-Being over Time in Britain and the USA," *Journal of Public Economics* 88 (2002): 1359–86.

22. Myrna Weissman, Martha Livingston Bruce, Philip J. Leaf, Louise P. Florio, and Charles Holzer III, "Affective Disorders," in *Psychiatric Disorders in America: The Epidemiologic Catchment Area Study*, eds. Lee N. Robins and Darrel A. Regier (New York: Free Press, 1991), 53–80; Cross-National Collaborative Group, "The Changing Rate of Major Depression: Cross-National Comparisons," *Journal of the American Medical Association* 268 (1992): 3098–105.

23. Alexis de Tocqueville, *Democracy in America*, ed. Phillips Bradley (1835; reprint New York: A.A. Knopf, 1945), 106. Citations from the Knopf edition.

Chapter 9: Social Disconnection and the Mental Health Industry

1. Rose J. Amanda, Wendy Carlson, and Erika M. Waller, "Prospective Associations of Co-Rumination with Friendship and Emotional Adjustment: Considering the Socio-Emotional Trade-Offs of Co-Rumination," *Developmental Psychology* 43 (2007): 1019–31.

2. Sarah W. Tracy, "Medicalizing Alcoholism One Hundred Years Ago," *Harvard Review of Psychiatry* 15 (2007): 86–91.

3. Ibid.

4. Michelle B. Cororve and David H. Gleaves, "Body Dysmorphic

Disorder: A Review of Conceptualizations, Assessment, and Treatment Strategies," *Clinical Psychology Review* 21 (2001): 949–70.

5. Bruce E. Wampold, *The Great Psychotherapy Debate: Models, Methods, and Findings* (Mahwah, NJ: Lawrence Erlbaum Associates, 2001), 58–71.

6. Richard S. Schwartz, "Psychotherapy and Social Support: Unsettling Questions," *Harvard Review of Psychiatry* 13 (2005): 272–79.

7. Richard S. Schwartz, "Psychotropic Goals: Normalization versus Enhancement," paper presented at American Psychiatric Association annual meeting, Philadelphia, 1994.

8. Michael Terman and Jiuan Su Terman, "Light Therapy for Seasonal and Nonseasonal Depression: Efficacy, Protocol, Safety, and Side Effects," *CNS Spectrums* 10 (2005): 647–63.

Chapter 10: Staying Limber

1. Stephanie Rosenbloom, "A Beautiful Day in the Neighborhood," *New York Times*, April 29, 2007.

2. Jean Kalata, "Looking at Act II of Women's Lives: Thriving and Striving from Forty-five On," *AARP Foundation Women's Leadership Circle Study* (Washington, DC: AARP, 2006).

3. Teach for America, "2007 Alumni Social Impact Report," www.teachforamerica.org/mission/our_impact/documents/ASIR.FINAL.Color_001.pdf.

4. Robert D. Putnam, *Bowling Alone: The Collapse and Revival of American Community* (New York: Touchstone, 2000), 394.

5. Jeff Miranda, "Take the Couch: Site Links Travelers, Hosts in the Spirit of Community," *Boston Globe*, August 22, 2007.

6. Putnam, *Bowling Alone*, 407.

7. Jacqueline Olds, Richard S. Schwartz, Susan Eisen, R. William Betcher, and Anthony Van Niel, "Part-Time Employment and Marital Well-Being: A Hypothesis and Pilot Study," *Family Therapy* 20 (1993): 1–16.

8. George Vaillant, "What Spirituality Is Good For: The Neurobiology of the Positive Emotions," grand rounds, McLean Hospital, May 10, 2007.

9. Putnam, *Bowling Alone*, 79.

10. Jo Williams, "Innovative Solutions for Averting a Potential Resource Crisis—the Case of One-Person Households in England and Wales," *Environment, Development and Sustainability* 9 (2007): 325–54.

11. William Kilpatrick, *Why Johnny Can't Tell Right from Wrong* (New York: Touchstone, 1992), 201.

12. Ibid.

13. Leon Wieseltier, *Kaddish* (New York: Vintage Books, 2000), 40.

Index